DG
78
M3
1963
glas

McDaniel, Walton Br
Roman private life
and its survivals.

GENESEE ABBEY LIBRARY
PIFFARD, N.Y. 14533 31149

GENESEE ABBEY LIBRARY
PIFFARD, N.Y. 14533

Our Debt to Greece and Rome

EDITORS

GEORGE DEPUE HADZSITS, PH.D.

DAVID MOORE ROBINSON, PH.D., LL.D.

ROMAN PRIVATE LIFE AND ITS SURVIVALS

BY

WALTON BROOKS McDANIEL, Ph.D.

COOPER SQUARE PUBLISHERS, INC.

NEW YORK

1963

Published 1963 by Cooper Square Publishers, Inc.
59 Fourth Avenue, New York 3, N. Y.
Library of Congress Catalog Card No. 63-10285

PRINTED IN THE UNITED STATES OF AMERICA
by SENTRY PRESS, NEW YORK, N. Y. 10013

CONTENTS

PREFACE

A WRITER who should attempt to show the influence of Roman private life upon the modern world would have to unite a specialist's familiarity with antiquity with a wide knowledge of the intervening centuries through which that influence might be traced. In addition, he ought to have spent at least one normal lifetime in each of the Latin countries. In these, at any rate, survivals are more easily detected and their history more definitely determined. Now, inasmuch as the editors' chance of finding a Methuselah possessed of such a combination of erudition and experience seemed somewhat remote, they had to seek as their alternative someone who had specialized in the field of private antiquities and yet would have the complaisance, or, if you will, the temerity to undertake a task of only less effrontery than that which the scheme of the Series seems primarily to demand. One might conceivably tell the tale of Roman life within the compass of a small book for general readers and at the same time indicate certain parallels between the life of antiquity and that of today which might or might not be an unbroken tradition from that remote period. To this lesser task the author has reluctantly directed his feeble powers; for the goddesses Πειθώ and Suada both intervened to his undoing. Fortunately during more than twenty-five years he had devoted many visits and several considerable stays in Latin countries to the collection of parallels between the present and the past. How little can be accomplished by a foreigner in such a period, even though he travels extensively and lives among the ordinary people with the set purpose of making his observations and collections, needs no other demonstration than this little treatise affords.

If the author has limited his sources almost entirely to Italy, it is because there the material is more abundant and instructive, and because he hoped that his love for a country that he regards almost as a second home might assure him an especial insight. A sympathetic appreciation of such a responsive race as the Italian will at any rate spare an investigator certain blunders of interpretation and grant him opportunities to learn that are denied the captious and the squeamish. That I have escaped all errors of understanding even in the limited selection that I have made from my collections is unlikely. To Commendatore H. Blakiston Wilkins of Florence and his family I am indebted for passing critically upon much of this manuscript; their knowledge of Italian life is so unusual as to constitute a valuable protection for one attempting my treacherous task.

Scholars writing for ordinary readers will always disagree as to the amount of space to be assigned various topics in what is at best a hopelessly brief account of Roman private life, nor can any writer, congesting the data of various periods to form a composite picture to fit the generations just before and just after the birth of Christ, avoid generalizations that he himself knows perfectly well are open to debate. That, however, makes the work of the reviewer easier, and one must be kind even to reviewers.

But even if one avoids anachronisms, there is still the danger that statements may be true of only a portion of the people at any given time. This book deals in the main with the life of the upper classes of the capital of the Roman world, the people with whom the student of Roman art and literature is chiefly concerned. The extent that the excavations of Ostia and Pompeii serve even this purpose needs no discussion here. The book might well accompany the visitor to such ruins, if he has no better help; but neither he nor the lover of Roman literature should expect from it any interpretation of the inner life of the ancient people. It deals primarily with the material existence and not with the thoughts and feelings of the Romans. It is bad enough to picture wrongly, as all writers are sure at times to do, the externals of ancient life; to misrepresent the spirit is worse. And finally some may wish that the author had put his material into the dramatic, story-book form which others with ampler space at their command have adopted. It seemed, however, preferable to compact the multitudinous facts into a booklet that should be serviceable to those, for instance, who read their Classics in the Translations of *The Loeb Classical Library*, rather than to essay any special entertainment of such readers as might never have grown up.

ROMAN PRIVATE LIFE AND ITS SURVIVALS

ROMAN PRIVATE LIFE
AND ITS SURVIVALS

I. THE HOME

FIRST of all we may turn our attention to the sort of habitation into which the Roman of our sketch might be born. The ordinary style of house construction used in Italy has depended upon factors some of which, such as climate and available building materials, have varied but little in thousands of years, while others have changed with the increasing complexity of civilization and the general advance in inventions throughout the world. The survivals from Roman times, however, seem to the Classicist who looks for them in his travels through the peninsula surprisingly numerous.

Our museums contain cinerary urns which Italians of prehistoric ages who practiced cremation of their dead fashioned to resemble the homes of the living. These hut urns acquaint us with a form of single-room dwelling, at first round, later oval, and eventually rectangular, built with wattled walls and a roof of thatch, and entered and often wholly lighted by a single door, the like of which may still be seen in many parts of Italy. For example in any *capanna* on Monte Circeo the birds whose crowing at the dawn of day's fostering light roused Evander from his humble home would find the same cock-roost that Virgil had in mind as he penned his verses in the *Aeneid*, as I can attest from having taken shelter in just such a wigwam after the owner with a delicate sense of hospitality had first ejected the family pig. The furnishing of the dim interior reminded me of the time when the Roman household dwelt in such a single room, with that promiscuous intimacy that poverty-stricken districts of Italy still exemplify. A central fireplace served for cooking, for the sacrificial offerings of religion, and, one might add, to keep the eyes moist with tears; for the smoke had only a small aperture in the roof or, in default of that, the open door through which to waft both the savor of food and the breath of prayer. Around this hearth the women would do their spinning and weaving, if the rain denied them the more agreeable workshop of all outdoors. Hard pallet beds at night received the tired household, who could have been no more fastidious about ventilation, smells and insects than their pastoral descendants of the twentieth century.

Theorizing about the development of this primitive cabin into the comfortable dwelling of the middle-class people which we find so well preserved at Pompeii and have reason to believe was usual in Rome also, raises debatable questions that stir pleasantly the acrimony of scholars but need no discussion here.

The ground floor plan of the type of Pompeian house that should chiefly interest the general reader is double. The front or *atrium*-half of the edifice is probably of Etruscan origin, the back undoubtedly of Greek. The houses were built to the street-line with no front or side yard anywhere. Their stucco façades were broken with relatively few and small windows, for the most part in the second story or high above the reach of thieves in the first. Balconies or bays often overhung from the upper floor, as we are now learning from the recent excavations at Pompeii. The

entrance door was commonly at the end of a
shallow vestibule. Thus the entire house
seemed to be looking inward, while our ability
to roll much larger sheets of glass [1] enables
us to make dwellings that look outward
through ample windows and doors and even
through sun-parlors and glass conservatories.
To this architectural introspection is largely
due that air of Oriental seclusion which so
impresses a visitor to the ruins.

The forepart of our typical Pompeian home
consists of a rectangular hall into which open
rooms on either side that were originally used
for bed-chambers, but which with changing
customs often served as store rooms or for
other purposes. The farthest rooms from the
front entry on each side were the so-called
" wings." These *alae* resembled alcoves in
being without doors and wholly open to the
central hall. In the city mansions of the
nobility they might be used for the display
of the ancestral busts, in niches in their walls.
Directly opposite the entrance of the *atrium*
and also wholly open to it was a capacious

[1] Windows without panes of glass are a common sight
in south Italy as they were of old. In the thirteenth
century even palaces in northern Italy lacked glass. See
L. Reggiani, *Strenna Guastellese,* p. 3.

apartment. This the master of the house used as a reception-room and office. By its central position it commanded all the activities of the home. Among its furnishings was a strong-box or safe, firmly bolted to a base of cement. In this would be kept the valuables which we may now store away in safe-deposit vaults. The quality of the mosaic floor and of the mural paintings as well as of the draperies which might curtain both the front and a rear opening of this room marked it out as one of the handsomest in the whole building. Along its side ran the passage that connected the two divisions of the house, and the room parallel to it on either side was likely to be a dining-room with an entrance into the other half of the house.

The ceiling of the *atrium* regularly had a large rectangular opening through which rain would fall from the roofs of tile, sloping inward. The tiles were of precisely the same construction as those now in use in Italy wherever snow [2] does not make their weight insupportable nor earthquakes dangerous. The rain-hole let in considerable light and also

[2] As at Agerola some four thousand feet above the bay at Castellamare di Stabia, where the roofs of wood resemble the Swiss.

assured an abundance of soft water much appreciated for washing purposes. Its framework might have the support of four or more columns. These rose from the edge of a shallow basin which caught the supply of rain and let off the overflow through piping into large cisterns beneath the floor. The basin itself might be adorned with a fountain-jet in the middle or at the inner end, so that even on sunny days there would be that plash of falling water that Italians still love to have in the courtyards of their homes.

Just as today in any Italian palace the ground floor apartments facing the street may be devoted to business uses,[3] so at Pompeii even in finer residences the rooms on each side of the entrance passage were often shops, the wares of which might be supplied from workrooms in the dwelling itself. Their entire interior was exposed to view during the day and the counter edged the sidewalk so that customers could trade across it without entering. Since the front at night was protected by board shutters, a Pompeian business street would, therefore, again remind one of the

[3] For the Tuscan palace with its *canova* or *cantina* see L. Villari, *Italian Life in Town and Country*, p. 25.

Orient, although just such shops with overhead awnings are still common also in parts of Greece and Italy. At Palermo, for example, there is at least one street largely lined with tiny restaurants, the odors from which are free to pour up and down the crowded thoroughfare as an advertisement or as a warning to possible customers, an exact reproduction of the Pompeian cook shops. Dwellings without stoves and chimneys have been the rule in much of Italy from the beginning, and to have the cooking done away from home is still commonly a convenience if not a necessity. The shops often had a half-story or mezzanine floor to which stairs ascended at their rear. These are exactly duplicated also in the arrangements of small shops in Naples. The owner sleeps upstairs above his goods.

As the front apartments of the house derived their light and air almost wholly from the *atrium*-aperture, so those in the rear division depended upon a colonnaded, rectangular court which gives the name peristyle to this Greek portion of the dwelling. By superimposing another colonnade they could secure an open gallery to light and give access to the upstairs rooms. These apartments in large houses might be let to lodgers as flats. The court was normally laid out in flower-beds and embellished by garden-statuary, fountain-basins, and in the middle a deep pool with a central fountain, an enviable provision for the small boy who here had none of the handicaps of hampering clothing and fussy parents that prevent the happy conversion of a bath-tub into an ocean of ships. Open courts are, of course, no rarity in Mediterranean lands today, where their combination of fresh air and sunshine with privacy are duly valued.

Around this *patio* the Pompeian located the more domestic apartments, the dining-rooms,[4] kitchen, larder, water-closet, bath and cells for the slaves. Here, too, might be the stable with no more regard for hygiene than in many an Italian *locanda* where the guests have only a floor or wall between them and the stalls. The family sleeping-chambers would be in the peristyle, either in the first or in a second story. Such a second floor in fact might be

---

[4] The ancient use of different dining-rooms and bed-chambers according to the exposure to the sun which summer or winter made desirable anticipates a practice of modern times in Venetian palaces. See W. D. Howells, *Venetian Life*, 2nd. Ed., pp. 41 and 391.

built over single rooms or groups of rooms in any part of the house; for the ancient architect was as indifferent to filling out, so to speak, the various strata of a dwelling as he was to making all parts of the same story of equal height. There are sometimes three or four levels in the lower story at Pompeii; but the rooms generally remind us of modern Italian apartments in being high-studded. This accords with an architectural tradition that has never lapsed, that dwellings should be built with a view to comfort rather in summer than in winter. To kiln-dried Americans a winter in sunny Italy is an Arctic experience. But we must not forget that in much of it there are really two winters, one of chill and rain, and a second, a " summer-winter " that for three or four months almost suspends outdoor work of man and beast by the severity of its heat.

In the peristyle portion of the house were also located some of the finest apartments for social purposes, beautified by superior mural paintings and by carefully laid mosaic floors. Luxurious residences might also include separate rooms for works of art and a library furnished with cases to contain the parchment

and papyrus rolls and with statues and busts
to indicate the occupant's esthetic and literary
predilections. Even the sun-parlor is no new
invention, nor is the value of a bath in it as
a therapeutic agent appreciated for the first
time in these days. During the winter period
Romans used to resort to a roof terrace (like
the aerial gardens that are so common on
Italian houses wherever the climate permits),
an open *loggia*, or some other basking-place,
with the same pleasure that they took in
going to their cold water bath during tropical
heat. At the rear of the house there was in
some cases a garden plot for the cultivation
of ornamental vegetation or of useful vegetables, nor must we forget that a dwelling
often had the enlargement of extra *atria* and
peristyles.

The kitchen deserves a special word not
only because it was likely to contain a shrine
for the household gods instead of being as now
in the United States the profanest apartment
of the house, but because the hearth arrangements are easily duplicated in contemporary
Italy. A fire of charcoal is nested in cavities
in the upper surface of what we might call a
range. Where wood was plentiful the ancients

kindled faggots on the hearth. The mere sight of such a contracted kitchen and primitive cooker, if in fact the smoke struggling for an exit through some hole [5] in the wall vouchsafed any eyesight at all, would put our pampered servants to a speedy flight. Of course, the Romans did their best with charcoal and with a specially prepared smokeless wood to minimize the fumes. What that best was can be surmised from the miracle that the poor of Italy still perform with incredibly little fuel and a fan to keep it hot.

We have now described in briefest outline the ordinary home of a prosperous Pompeian. But it is needless to say that at Rome there were not only dwellings similar to these but also private residences of the wealthy, the lofty halls and magnificent courts of which can best be imagined after a visit to the ruins of the imperial palaces themselves. In such, for instance, the vestibule becomes a portico with sculpture and other splendid adornment, while the marble veneering of wall surfaces all over the building can be adequately ap-

[5] We can allow neither Shakespeare in his *Julius Caesar* nor Sienkiewicz in his *Quo Vadis* to picture chimneys on the dwellings of ancient Rome. They are still rare in many Italian communities.

preciated only after one has seen the finer churches of Rome which owe their beauty to transfers of ancient splendor.

There were also at the capital abodes of wretchedness, great tenement houses, so poorly constructed that their tumbling was no phenomenal event. Being bounded by four streets, they were called "islands," *insulae*. Like the huge lodging houses of Naples they might have a single shrine for the worship of the entire tenantry. The inhabitants certainly needed the unifying influence of religion as much as do those of the *bassi* and of the still worse *fondachi* today. A large family might eat, sleep and slave in a single room or in a few-room flat, in the same demoralizing congestion as there used to be in the rookeries of American cities before restrictive building laws were passed and inspectors ceased to wink. In ancient Rome also legislation fixed the maximum height of buildings, now at seventy feet and again at sixty, but even edifices of the former limit would hardly qualify as modern skyscrapers. Of lodging houses of the superior sort the newer excavations at Ostia are now giving us some idea. They seem very modern.

[14]

A superficial observer at Pompeii is likely
to exclaim: " Here certainly every man's
house is his castle," but the privacy must
have been only apparent. While there would
be no embarrassment from strangers staring
through windows on the street, the ancients
were sometimes troubled by having their
neighbors peer from above through the rain-
hole of the *atrium* or into the peristyle court.
The former, indeed, had to be closed with a
grating as a protection against descending
thieves, quite as we might safeguard a sky-
light. Moreover, the abundance of domestic
slaves speaking a Babel of different tongues
inevitably caused noise and confusion. In
big establishments we hear of special " silence
makers," *silentarii,* " mufflers " we might call
them, who were expected to keep their fellow-
servants quiet, and we can well understand
why literary workers were inclined to seek
the calmer and ampler quarters of their
country villas.

So far as interior decoration is concerned,
the mosaic pavements, fresco-paintings and
plastic work in stucco which delight the artistic visitor to Pompeii were naturally carried
to higher perfection in the nobler mansions

of the capital, but their wide-spread use in the little Campanian town evidences an esthetic interest upon the part of the masses of which Italians still have some right to boast. Their fondness for work in plaster, for marble and for fresco-painting is a long tradition: the best that they do is still unsurpassed.

II. FURNITURE

ANCIENT furniture was notable more for the artistic taste and costly materials displayed in its construction than for its abundance and comfort. Even now Italy has no such exacting cult of ease and convenience as is general in the United States. But the carving of the furniture and the inlaid work in ivory, metal and tortoise-shell already gave promise of what our Italian craftsman can do with these materials. To be sure, anciently the inspiration and much of the workmanship were probably Greek. The larger pieces in the home of the upper classes comprised their rather high beds, low dinner-sofas, reading and writing couches, chairs, stools, tables, chests, upright cabinets or cupboards, and a cradle for the never-failing baby. Minor articles included writing implements and materials,[6] the same sort of child's saving bank [7] that encourages thrift

[6] Already in Ovid's day lovers were using invisible inks to protect their billets-doux from prying eyes.

[7] Those found at Pompeii resemble closely the *carusedda* or *salvadanai* of the Sicilians as they are pictured by

today, musical instruments, the lyre, the pipes, the tambourine, and among the rich even a water-organ. Nor must we leave out the bag-pipe which is still a favorite among the peasants of Sicily. In various parts of Italy it has long been played with the *piffero,* or pastoral pipe, before the street-shrines of the Madonna in the Christmas season, with the same spirit of homage that in Ovid's day inspired the devotees of the Mother of the Gods to shrill their horns before her. Lighting and heating required lanterns, lamps,[8] candelabra and portable braziers which were precisely like those in common use in the great galleries and palaces of Italy — memorials rather than producers of heat one might call them. For kindling the hearth they used fire-sticks or the flint and steel, together with sulphured matches and other tinder. Then there were sun-dials and now and then a water-clock which worked on the principle of our hour-glasses. We may add to our list the

G. Pitré, *Catalogo Illustrato della Mostra Etnografica Siciliana* (1892), p. 39, No. 118.

[8] Inscriptions on some wishing the owner a "Happy New Year" make them seem like our modern presents for that season. Olive oil is still burned in country districts in lamps of much the same shape as those of two thousand years ago.

toilet articles,[9] including such refinements as tooth-picks, ear-picks, nail files and hair tweezers; the domestic equipment for cleansing, such as brooms, brushes and sponges; the cooking and eating utensils, not overlooking such niceties as cake moulds and egg beaters and a nursing bottle for the baby; and finally articles used in exercise and for the bath. In what category one should place the back-scratcher may be dubious, but its utility is obvious to anyone who knows Italian hexapods. Our long list reads much more like the equipment of a modern house than the layman might have imagined.

One piece of silver plate even a poor family might own, the salt-cellar, containing the important ingredient of the *mola salsa* or sacrificial cake. Even yet it has hardly lost its ranking position of all the tableware. Of course, the wealthy vied with one another in the possession of vessels of costly metal and of artistic beauty. Extant specimens almost justify envy. Another token of wealth, the

[9] The hair-pin had but a single prong and might be adorned at the other end with the representation of a hand the outstretched fingers of which were supposed to avert the evils of witchcraft. South Italian and Sicilian women display the same type to this day.

Oriental rug, was not yet in use on Italian floors, but curtains, spreads and draperies were a common importation from the East long before imperial times.

Only persons of means, especially in the more northern provinces of the empire, would have hot-air heating systems for the living rooms of the house, but everywhere bath apartments depended upon a furnace to send warmth through register-like openings into a chamber, or more commonly, to circulate it through double walls and hollow floorings. In general Italians still prefer the gratuitous but fitful heat of the sun to the costly emanations of a fuel fire.

Water was piped into the dwellings from a city supply brought in by aqueducts and distributed by city mains. Some of these aqueducts are still in use in whole or in part. To secure pressure, water towers were used, such as may still be seen in Palermo, for instance, as well as in ancient Pompeii. Cisterns for rain water were also a dependence, as they still are in more waterless sections of the peninsula. The poor had to resort, of course, to street fountains, as in most Italian communities of today. The carrying of water jars on

their heads has made living caryatides of
Italian girls for thousands of years. The
young mother was and is at her prettiest when
balancing in a basket on her head her chubby
baby, lulled to slumber by the swaying
movement.

Amulets were also among the furnishings of
an ancient home. Not a few will still catch
the eye of a keen observer in humbler dwellings of Italy. While two millennia ago the
superstitious warded off the maleficence of
magic by making finger-signs that Italians
still use against a momentary danger, yet permanent charms on one's person [10] or on one's
possessions would seem to have advantages
over any temporary gesture. Thus, on the
homeopathic principle perhaps of using like
versus like, a representation of the human
eye was frequently to be found on all sorts of
objects, especially upon pottery. If the evil
eye really has anything to do with the smash-

[10] A Neapolitan professor of the Classics introduced
himself to one of my students to inquire what sort of
amulet his Phi Beta Kappa key was. Trinkets that represent the sign of the " horns " or of the " fig " have
several millennia of precedents behind them; so, too, the
sea-horse or hippocamp in the neighborhood of Naples,
although now it is outranked in popularity by the *cima-
ruta* and *sirena*.

ing of our household china, we may well redecorate both cook and kitchen. The grotesque, the comical and the obscene were particularly efficacious against the glance of envy or of any other evil influence, catching it and averting it, one might say, as a lightning rod the thunderbolt. We must not, therefore, draw wrong conclusions [11] from the presence on Pompeian houses of symbols that we deem indecent to a degree. The practice is not quite dead yet in that region, but none the less the people using such safeguards are and were quite respectable.

[11] As, for instance, André Maurel, *A Fortnight in Naples,* translated by H. Gerard, p. 211, misjudges the famous house of the Vettii at Pompeii, which has a shocking *fora-fascino* at the very front door.

III. THE HOUSEHOLD

WE must next occupy ourselves with the men, women and children who dwelt in this home. From our point of view, they would seem to overcrowd it. The Latin noun from which our word family is derived might be better represented in English by the term "house" or "household"; for, especially among the earlier Romans, several generations of the same lineage often lived together in the same abode. Similarly today in Italy, two or three sets of husband, wife and children will dwell under the same roof-tree, and the expression *la mia famiglia* includes the servants. Clannishness and nepotism are the natural result of this intra-mural intimacy, and were in evidence anciently.

The *paterfamilias* or head of the house would be the oldest of the fathers. Subject absolutely to his power, whether they abode in his home, or, as sometimes happened in the case of his descendants, elsewhere, would be not only his own wife and their unmarried children, but also his married sons, whether by birth or by adoption, together with their wives and all the next generations on the same principle, so long as he lived. A maiden daughter escaped his rule only by becoming a Vestal Virgin (not exactly an ancient nun, since she could wed after thirty years) or by marrying into a similar absolutism in another family; a son by becoming a special priest, or by a complicated legal process of emancipation. Not at all unlike this system is the government of many a large group of kinspeople in Tuscany today where the *capoccio* or head man and the *massaia* or house-mother settle everything from business to matrimony, the ultimate word, however, resting with the male, as it did with Adam until Eve was born.

The importance of this household hegemony and of the perpetuation of the family can hardly be overestimated. The Roman thought of the spirits of the dead as hovering around the spot where their mortal relics lay, dependent for their felicity upon regular offerings of food and drink to be given them by their survivors. In default of descendants or of those who acted in their capacity, the dead were doomed to a joyless existence which might easily turn them into demons full of malice towards the world. On the other hand, souls that were well treated would keep watch and ward over their benefactors. To be childless, therefore, was to be accursed; not to marry was to defraud generations of ancestors of their due. However burdensome, marriage was less an evil than that which it sought to avoid. If it proved to be barren, the husband could yet fulfill his religious obligations to the dead by choosing one of two alternatives: he might have himself adopted into another family where there were heirs or — the preferable method — himself adopt a son.

The absolute power that the head of a house could exercise over his dependants not only gave him the complete disposal of all property that they might earn or acquire, but even permitted him to decide whether a new-born baby should be deprived of life or reared, whether a penalty for disobedience should be some mild punishment or (at least in early days) enslavement, banishment or death. Of course, in actual practice we must not think of the Romans as either robbing or killing members of their own family. The *paterfa-*

milias was rather a judge with invited assessors than a practising tyrant. Even the law gradually set some restrictions, and public opinion always imposed restraints. Just as in France the question of a divorce, as involving not merely a couple but all their connections, calls for a family council, so among the ancient Romans not only divorce but all severer punitory measures required the summoning of friends and relatives to consider the justice and advisability of them, the Italian *consiglio di famiglia*. The life of the home was apparently no more contentious than it averages today, but the respect for elders and especially for parents would seem to us more Chinese than American.

The one human element that was responsible perhaps for the greatest difference between our life and that of antiquity was the slave. To him we must now devote a major amount of attention. An American visiting the homes of well-to-do families in Italy and to a less degree living in the more pretentious hotels of that country is impressed by the minute division of labor among the servants and by their consequent excess in number. Tasks of outdoor work also employ what seems to us far too many hands. One might imagine that the economic conditions of the present had never diverged much from those traditional in the days of human slavery. To be sure, the first Romans had no such superfluity of unpaid assistance as wealthier citizens of the Empire were to have. It was not, indeed, until the conquests of the second century B.C. had brought countless prisoners of war in servitude to Rome that the institution of slavery got its strangle-hold upon the people. Thenceforth there was an increasing degradation of free labor. By the close of the Republic, in fact, all manual occupations, most of the trades and even some of what we now term the professions, such as medicine and surgery, were largely in the hands of slaves and ex-slaves, and it meant social debasement for a freeman of birth and education to compete with them, even if he could with any financial profit.

We cannot deal here with the larger economic changes, the diminution and practical disappearance of a middle class, the enlistment of potentially productive thousands in the army, the increase of the idle protelariat concentrated in the cities and more especially in the capital, calling for *panem et circenses,* " free bread and the games of the circus," quite as more recent commoners have insisted on having their three F's, *festa, fuoco* (fireworks), *farina.*[12] We can only mention the fusion of small farms, once tilled by independent, self-respecting farmers, into enormous estates, worked by slaves and cursed by the same evils of absentee landlordism that Italy still exhibits on its *latifondi.* Nor can we discuss the lives and occupations of the numerous public slaves. We are rather concerned with the effect of slavery upon the individual home.

The personal attentions of ubiquitous, obsequious menials are sure in any age to impair the fibre of manhood and induce in womanhood false standards of luxury and pride. Roman children of sterling ancestry in the close confines of the home had constant and unescapable contacts with at least the alien and often the immoral ideas and conduct of men and women debased by servitude. Slaves had every inducement to pamper their young charges and encourage an egotism that spells

[12] The maxim of Lorenzo the Magnificent ran: *Pane e feste tengon il popol quieto.*

ruin. While there were thousands of families where there would be no slave or possibly only one, as soon as you reached the level of what would be called polite society, there was a different tale to tell, particularly during the early Empire. Then even a modest establishment needed a minimum of ten servants to meet the requirements of gentility and a real palace might house its hundreds.[13] To have the same person serving as major domo and cook called forth the sneers of a Cicero. Gossips asked not " How much money is so and so worth? " but " How many slaves does he keep? "

In the larger mansions the army of domestics had to be divided into squads of ten, each with its own supervisor, and that master had, indeed, a retentive memory who could call by name a majority of his own servitors. Under these circumstances a certain absence of sympathy was inevitable, although for the most part self-interest and the requirements of peace and quiet in such a crowded household

[13] Those who have kept house under the somewhat similar conditions that minute division of labor creates in contemporary Italian households sense the full significance of the proverb: *qui vuol esser mal servito, tenga assai famiglia.*

made the Roman master accord his domestic workers tolerable treatment, while his own body-servants and private secretary might command from him a sincere affection. The enfranchisement of a slave girl in order to marry her was not at all unheard of among decent people. Instances of loyalty and devotion parallel those of aged retainers [14] in certain Italian families of today, not to speak of house-servants in our own South before the Civil War.

While a hundred dollars, the wages of a few weeks of recalcitrant, unskilled labor in our kitchens, would buy outright a competent manual laborer in Rome of two millennia ago, thousands were necessary to secure a fancy article, a handsome boy to wait at table, a girl to sing or play the lyre on occasion but to look pretty all the time, or even — such was the Roman discernment of real worth! — a grammarian, a eunuch or a fool.

Both the elementary school teacher and the *paedagogus* or tutor who helped the boy with

[14] The attitude of servants is, however, changing so rapidly in Italy that such relationships as *e.g.* M. Carmichael, *In Tuscany,* pp. 6, 49 ff., 58 ff., and 67, pictures with delightful charm, will soon be known only in novels of the past.

his lessons and chaperoned him from morn till night were likely to be Greek slaves. In controlling their charges these men had to depend on corporal punishment rather than upon moral suasion; for children soon learned the normal Roman's ill-concealed contempt for the people across the Adriatic. This method of foreignizing youth is perpetuated in our age by the system of governesses. Moreover, the unmarried Italian girl of social standing is still never to be seen unaccompanied on the streets. It is quite possible, too, that if she had the middle-class privilege of going to school with her brothers, some attendant might carry her lesson books, as in the good old days of Rome. So firm stands the fabric of social convention against the seismic shocks of progress!

Slaves who had been trained to various arts and crafts were often a source of income to their owner, who let them out to those who stood in need of their skill or labor or lent them capital to conduct a business of their own. Experienced slaves also kept the accounts of the household, superintended the shops or workrooms and labored in them, bought the daily provisions and the more permanent supplies, no small task where there were so many to feed and clothe, and when there were no department stores like ours providing anything from a needle to a carriage. Furthermore, every branch of the household economy had to have its own specialist, the kitchen, dining-rooms, and bed-chambers. The very house door would prepare you for what you would note inside; for there was the tiny office of a slave who had naught to do but guard the entrance, the prototype of the modern porter,[15] but, unlike him, sometimes chained to his post to insure his presence. The toilet of the ladies demanded the skill of experts too numerous to list, but husband and children were hardly less exacting in their needs of specialists to cut and dress their hair, bathe and clothe their persons, and answer every beck and call as errand boys.

Fashion prescribed a retinue of servants on the streets, even if one were not borne along in a litter, shaded by sun-umbrellas, paged by handsome boys and cooled by fans of palm

[15] This functionary, humble and yet all-powerful either to vex or to serve and please, is likely nowadays to carry on some petty supplementary employment while seated at the entrance, such as the repairing of shoes or the vending of flowers.

leaf or of peacock plumes, held in the hands
of flunkies. So travelled the rich, who gave
to the liveries of their bearers and to the
comfort of their litters the same attention that
the privileged few can still give to the equipment of their sedans and limousines. A trip
out of the city set a small army of servants
on the march, carriage drivers and outriders,
persons to care for the baggage in the wagons
and on the beasts of burden, not to mention
in some cases private soldiery, a band of
gladiators to protect the traveller against
bandits or against the similar bravos of their
political opponents. There were, to be sure,
those like Horace and like many a happy but
hardy tourist of today who could travel long
distances on donkey back with the nuisance
of but few attendants, but such was not the
liberty of the social élite of Rome at the beginning of our era. Nor can we omit from
our enumeration a whole class of ancient servitors whose modern representatives must be
seen chiefly on the vaudeville stage, at the
circus or in some museum. We refer to those
slaves whose personal oddities or deformities,[16]

[16] One of the most persistent traits in Italian character seems to be their sense of the ridiculous. They
have always been prone to personalities, quick to coin

gifts of comic speech or action, or musical or histrionic ability made them welcome entertainers at dinner parties. They might be of either sex and of any age, and their performances ran from the level of obscenities and vulgarities such as now enthrall our lowest audiences to the highest reaches of dramatic art, to the reading, for instance, of a masterpiece of literature to a group of cultivated gentlemen.

Slaves constituted such a considerable element of the populace that the life they led and the treatment they received is of concern to any student of antiquity. Within recent years labor has won so much from capital and working conditions in most civilized countries have been so bettered that we may find difficulty in visualizing the lot to which a slave was born or to which a foreigner might be reduced through financial adversity or the vicissitudes of war. A marked difference in color and civilization separated our recent slaveholders from their human chattels. Among them there was more irony but less

apt nicknames and tolerant of both. Barbieri would have been called by the Latin equivalent of Guercino and Barbarelli by that of Giorgione, had they lived in Roman days.

cruelty in christening a negro " Caesar " or
" Pompey " than in re-naming a Greek prisoner
of war " Croesus " after his enslavement by
some Roman who was his inferior in birth,
breeding and education.

Of course, some slaves were born to servitude, others owed their fate to punishment
for having tried to escape some civic duty or
for having played the " slacker " in time of
war. By the first century A.D. Romans were
securing their chief supply of them through
purchase in the open market, where they would
be exposed naked on the auction platform to
be duly handled, trotted about, and tested by
the prospective purchaser; for even a professional swapper of horses might learn from
these ancient dealers how to conceal infirmi-
ties and inefficiencies.

Chalked feet meant that the slave was
newly imported, holes in his ears that he was
an Oriental, a label hung round his neck that
he was warranted, a cap on his head that he
was not. The points usually covered by the
guarantee were that he was sound of mind
and body, with no tendency to epilepsy or
suicide, nor propensity to thieve or run away.

A slavemaster's power was absolute. Significant is an ancient classification of agricultural instruments into those that are "mute," such as the plough, "semi-vocal," as the ox, and "vocal," as the slave. The bondsman was merely a "living tool." [17] Even the union of slaves as man and wife lacked sanctity and stability. The children born were liable to be sold to a distance, as in our own country before the Civil War. On the other hand, those home-born slaves were most usually, as being the close associates of the master's own youngsters, a petted and pampered lot. The money that a slave could scrape together was his by courtesy rather than by any legal right. The man who owned him body and soul could deprive him of the savings of a lifetime for any sort of guilt. Fortunately it was so desirable to cultivate frugality and cheerful obedience in a domestic by giving him something to live for that his small funds were usually safe and might enable him eventually to buy either freedom from his owner or a

[17] There is a sad parallel to this in the life of the *guitti,* the "dirty ones," who live in the primitive huts of the Campagna, as the reader will find it movingly set forth in A. Cervesato, *The Roman Campagna,* translated by L. Caico and M. Dove, pp. 179 ff. Old Cato would have made an effective *caporale.*

slave of his own. The lot of this slave of a slave proverbially resembled that of the workman of today who serves under a boss who was once in the same condition.[18]

A slave's punishment for real or fancied offenses might range from a simple lashing to an ignominious death and a forgotten burial. We find in use prototypes of the modern "stocks," in which the inability of the victim even to move exposed him to the vilification and tormenting of those who joy in badgering so long as it be safe. A transfer from urban service to the gruelling labor of a farm, a grain-mill or a stone quarry was also a dreaded threat. On big estates the field hands often had to work in fetters, and only confinement at night in semi-underground barracks could insure their presence in the morning for further fagging toil. The chance to make an escape even in a crowded city with open country about was poor. In an age that knew no abolitionists, self-interest turned everybody's hands against the fugitive, and professional slave-hunters had plenty of volunteers to help them. With unconscious humor a runaway

[18] As the Spanish proverb puts it: *contra peon hecho dama no para pieza en tabla.*

was said to have stolen himself. Recapture resulted in branding on the forehead with F, the initial letter of the Latin word for fugitive, and in maltreatment more dreadful than death.

Nor was the revenge of murdering a master so sweet as to be worth the risk of crucifixion, the most agonizing of all executions, which awaited his almost certain detection. Chronically refractory slaves were sometimes sold to gladiatorial schools where their brutality could be curbed and made valuable.

The food and clothing apportioned a slave would suffice to keep him efficient as a worker but no more. While denied, of course, the use of the dress of citizenship, slaves would look in general like the very poor among the free. History tells us of a bill in the senate which proposed to put them all in uniform, but it failed to pass, through fear that a recognition of their numerical preponderance would lead to dangerous uprising such as several times nearly wrecked the state anyway. There were, indeed, many masters who subscribed to the statement that a man had as many enemies as he had servitors.

It was only by stinting his appetite and selling from his rations that the slave saved what he was allowed to regard as his own. The self-indulgent were free to consume their scanty dole entirely and even to supplement it by tid-bits bought with such money as they received as presents or tips. For the origin of the tipping system can be traced at least as far back as the early Roman Empire, when even access to the lord of a mansion might be attainable only by judicious bribery of his servants, and other favors were equally purchasable. The food of the slave was probably no worse, at any rate, than that of the humble free, but it could be in painful contrast with the living which he had enjoyed before the lottery of war deprived him of native land and family, snapping every social, religious and moral tie for a desperate forever.

Of course, both Stoic teaching and the progress of Christianity gradually ameliorated the condition of the slaves. In all periods, masters were conferring freedom upon them, changing them from " things " to " persons " as a reward for lengthy fidelity or for some special act of merit. As a freedman, he remained still in a state of semi-dependence upon his former master, whose relationship to him was now that of patron to client. They helped each other. The ex-slave might indeed conduct business enterprises for his former owner with money which the latter furnished as capital and enjoy a stipulated share in all profits. Freedmen became immensely wealthy as agents of men of senatorial rank, who could do no business that would take them out of Italy, and as household officials of the emperors. The administrative ability of freedmen, especially those of Greek stock, was a great asset to the government; but their rise to power in general was largely responsible for a materialism that was in painful contrast to the austere simplicity that had characterized the Republic nearly to its close.

The system of slavery brought its own punishment upon its upholders. Habitual exercise of arbitrary power and the self-indulgence that was fostered by luxuriously minute service led to that pride of despotism that is its own undoing. Slavery was one of the factors that brought the world's greatest empire tumbling to its fall.

IV. MATRIMONY

BEFORE we start a Roman baby on the career of manhood or womanhood, we had better wed its parents. The institution of matrimony enjoyed among the early Romans at least as much respect as it is now accorded in the United States, and no other people have ever regarded the rearing of children as more essential to the civic and religious interests of their state. But even if the oft-repeated statement were true that for five hundred years after the founding of the city there was no case of divorce, it would only seem remarkable if we could be sure that it was not rather the machinery for separation than a cause for it that was lacking. This is the vital point which it irks some reformers even now to recognize. Moreover, a Roman union was a *marriage de convenance,* so that, as in Latin countries still, the bride and groom often had to depend upon post-marital propinquity to develop a love that may safely be assumed to precede most American marriages.

We read of two methods of marrying, one by which the bride came into the complete power of her husband, " into his hand " the Latin phrase neatly puts it, and the other by which she remained under her father's control and retained any property of her own and the right to inherit from him. This latter method seems to have amounted to no more than the consent of the parties, without ceremony, to live with each other as man and wife, and it had become so popular by the close of the Republic as to make almost obsolete the following three forms which once enjoyed supreme importance though they subjected the wife wholly to her husband.

The most elaborate of the three was a sacramental ceremony, the confarreate wedding, which was so called because the couple ate together a cake of spelt (*far*), a sacred offering to Jupiter. Since presumably the god was once thought to reside in the cake, this was really a communion service as well as a mystical initiation of the woman into the religious life of her husband's family. As a matter of fact, the confarreate wedding was as impressive and binding as any that sacerdotalism has ever evolved. It was the exclusive privilege and affliction of patricians.

Another method of marrying, plebeian in its origin, was simpler, being effected by a fictitious sale of the bride to the groom in the presence of five witnesses and of a person who held a pair of scales, not as symbolizing the justice that should control matrimonial relations, but as a relic of the day when money was not minted and had to be weighed.

Simpler still and apparently the earliest was the third process of constituting wedlock which demanded nothing but a year of uninterrupted living together. Moreover, in this type of union, the wife might conserve her wedlock and yet continue under the same control as before marrying by merely absenting herself for a period of three nights in that annual term. In other words, this might be regarded as a sort of trial marriage to fix upon one's choice of *paterfamilias*.

A betrothal ceremony was in no wise obligatory, but became more and more fashionable under the Empire. We actually hear of marriage-brokers, such as still do business in Italian rural districts; but they could scarcely have been so effectively organized as European matrimonial bureaus are now under the joint patronage of Hymen and Plutus. Roman marriage lacked such preliminary of lovemaking and courtship as is normal in America (though still rare in much of Italy today), because boys and girls had almost no chance for intimate association except perhaps at public festivals. The arrangements were made by the fathers [19] or guardians of the couple, who might at the time be of any age over six. The future bridegroom was assured as large a dowry as the shrewdness of his father could exact, while there was a unilateral promise on the part of the girl that she would marry him. His pledge to her might be of iron, not in the metaphorical, but in the literal sense; for fashion long sanctioned an iron engagement ring that, so far as our literary evidence goes, seems to have lacked even a gem to embellish it. Professional jilts may ponder this pretty practice along with the humor of a certain Roman law that denied a

[19] Even among the Italians in an American city it may be a purely parental affair. The girl " often does not even know whom she is to marry until the matter is all settled; " cf. Park and Miller, *Old Traits Transplanted*, p. 156. Of course, the conditions in the old country are well known.

man who broke his engagement the recovery of his espousal gifts. However, the maiden did the best she could with her ring by wearing it on the third finger of her left hand from which it was believed a nerve ran straight to her heart. In later folklore this link is called not a sinew but the *vena amoris*. We hear of yet another law that prescribes marriage within two years, if the betrothal was to be valid, but it is obvious that the age of the betrothed must have been a factor in the length of the engagement.

While legally a girl could marry at twelve and a boy at fourteen, the girl usually waited to at least the latter age and the youth to his twenties. The disparity between their ages often meant a certain initial schooling of the girl by her mature husband as in similar Italian marriages in our time. If, however, a daughter had reached her latest teens with no sign of a suitor, she might be reckoned a little *passée*, and father and mother would incline to increase the amount of her dowry and let the new offering be known among prospective eligibles, lest she be doomed to an unlovely spinsterhood. Pagan Pliny's bestowal of marriage-portions on the poor set a precedent for philanthropy of the same sort in the Christian Italy that we know. As a matter of fact, unmarried women with records of long expectancy have always been as rare in that country as child-mothers are common, and among the ancient Romans they seem to have been as phenomenal as in all ages among the Jews.

For the marriage the question of lucky and unlucky days was quite as important as among the meticulous of today. There is a well known couplet:

> Nè di Venere nè di Marte
> Non si sposa, nè si parte

which attests the ban that is put on Tuesday and Friday. Again, the month of May is only preserving its old disrepute, while June, which is now in such high favor as " the month of brides," used to be in its first half just as bad as May. It was April that most enjoyed the grace of Venus. In all, a full third of the three hundred and sixty-five days was for one reason or another under the ban of Hymen.

Just as nowadays a profane Justice of the Peace in a bare office can tie as tight a matrimonial knot as an archbishop may with all the hallowed glory of a cathedral wedding, provided a certain minimum be done and spoken, so in Rome, after parental accord had been reached the only real essential was the consent of bride and groom to their contract. In the various forms of ceremony already described this could be symbolized by the joining of right hands in the presence of witnesses, or by the escorting of the bride to her husband's home in procession, or by the actual signing of a document, or by several of these acts combined. The noteworthy fact is that if the pair wished merely to be married, neither state nor religious authorities had to play a rôle, and the amount of fashionable embellishment was left to the individual taste and purse.

On the day before her wedding the maiden dedicated to deity her toys and her gown of childhood, — luckily not a limousine and a Worth frock! — Her bridal costume included a white tunic of an old-fashioned weave, girt with a woolen girdle which was tied with a " true lover's " knot of Hercules, a trusted protection against the magic of an envious glance. Her shoes were saffron yellow, her ample veil the color of flame. The latter was so characteristic of her trousseau that to "take the veil" in Latin meant for a woman to make the vows not of celibacy but of matrimony. The closest parallel for the headgear today is perhaps the flame-colored, gold-fringed veil that a Greek bride wears. In memory probably of an age when men consummated marriage by capturing their bride at the point of the spear (the practice ultimately responsible for the story of the rape of the Sabines), the groom in more civilized times used to divide the girl's hair into six tresses with the point of a spear-like implement. Above these, as arranged around her head, she wore a garland of flowers which she had plucked with her own hand. Her mate, too, might wear a chaplet.

The opening scene of the ceremonies was at the house of the bride's father, which would be adorned with flowers and shrubbery, as would also the home of the groom. Early on the morning of the wedding day, a professional diviner ascertained the omens. If there were a marriage contract, the witnesses to the signing would be ten. In confarreate and co-emption weddings the woman spoke an ancient formula of words that (using typical names, as we may say "John Doe") declared her

Gaia where or when her husband was Gaius. A matron friend of the bride next brought the two together for the solemn clasping of right hands. Prayer, sacrifices and wishes of good luck were then in order, and a wedding feast followed at which the guests received their portions of a wedding cake, the ingredients of which, anise, cumin, cheese, flour, lard and must, would promise little to a modern appetite, no matter how skilful the cooking may have been.

If the more ancient practices were followed, this brought the celebration to the fall of night. Then, just at the poetic hour when the evening star was rising (in notable contrast with the glare and hubbub of a modern high-noon wedding), the torch-light procession would form to escort the bride to her new home. Again in simulation of that primitive marriage by capture the girl was torn from her mother's arms with a feint of force.[20] Her escort, to the music of pipe players would include besides the guests the usual uninvited multitude of the curious. As the parade proceeded, there were cries to the marriage god,

[20] A show of violence is still the tradition in the marriage rites of Albanian communities of Italy; cf. Caterina Pigorini-Beri, *In Calabria*, 2nd. Ed., 1892, pp. 46–50.

much singing of coarse, satiric songs and a scrambling for nuts which the groom was expected to shower among the omnipresent small boys. Originally, like the rice that is thrown today, this fruit of a prolific tree symbolized fertility. The youngsters might save the nuts for use as marbles or stow them away at once where they would alleviate the gastric gnawings that boyhood never lacks.

The writer once saw a procession of a double wedding wending its way between the high walls of Anacapri's lanes, during which there was scrambling for candy nuts and many a sally from above, which sounded more profane than sacred and heightened the shy terror of at least the male half of the quartette. With the largess of nuts we may compare the *dragées* (boxes of candy-covered almonds) used in polite society in Italy for a wedding and in France for a Christening.

A page used to walk on each side of the bride, a third boy carried before her a torch of white thorn as an avertive of evil. For this there was a contest among the guests at the end of the ceremonies. They also displayed in the parade the girl's distaff and spindle. Having arrived at the house, she

anointed the door-posts with oil as a symbol
of fat days to come and wound them with
woolen fillets as a token of her own household
occupations, unless perhaps these acts were
merely dedicatory rites to deity. She made
her first entrance by being lifted over the
threshold, either to guard against the ill omen
of a stumble or as a reminiscence of the days
when exogamy even at the cost of violence
was the marriage practice and the bride went
in kicking and struggling in her captor's arms.
Here too she may have repeated the formula
which originally may have meant that thereafter her husband's name was to be her name,
but which sounds like a declaration of part-
nership. He now brought her symbolic gifts
of fire and water, while she, on her part, if
early customs were observed, presented him
with a bronze coin, a first payment on her
dowry, and the household gods with another,
having already bestowed a third upon the
deities of the neighboring crossways; nor did
she omit a prayer for marital happiness before the marriage couch, set in the *atrium*.
At a second wedding banquet which closed
the following day, she made her first sacrifice
to the gods as a Roman matron. In fashion-

able society the ensuing weeks would be full of dinner parties in honor of the newly wed.

Human nature was not supernatural in antiquity, and it cannot surprise us if marriages contracted largely at the invitation of others between those who were sometimes from our point of view mere children, had to be dissolved. Under the free forms that prevailed by the close of the Republic, a mere renouncement of the bond because of absence of marital affection was all that was necessary to legalize divorce, and there was some dispute as to whether even re-marriage alone would not do it. Notice would ordinarily be served, but sometimes the husband merely broke the marriage tablets, or taking the key turned his spouse out of the house. On the other hand, even the wife's *paterfamilias* long had the right to dissolve her union with her husband. Ultimately the law required seven witnesses for a repudiation document, and theoretically it always vetoed groundless separations and punished misconduct that justified a divorce.

However, as the Republic closed, dissolutions of marriage seem to have almost kept pace with the consummations. The family

life that was once Rome's best asset was now
sadly demoralized. Legislation displayed more
than its usual degree of impotence to mend
the people's morals. Of course, the satirists
revelled in the opportunities that are still offered the scandal-mongers of our "yellow
press," but we must exercise caution in ac-
cepting what they say as a fair statement of
the truth. Nor must we ignore in our judg-
ments the ancient point of view. Quite
respectable Romans reckoned concubinage
reputable and legitimate for the unmarried
man and, in general, the sexual relations of a
man with an alien woman or with a slave were
of minimum concern to polite society and none
at all to the State, since their offspring did
not figure as a citizen. A divorce was not a
disgrace; it was merely the dissolution of a
contract, and the dowry system made it unnecessary for any woman to live with a man she
hated merely in order to live at all. The continued importance of the *dot* among the Latin
races will not surprise anybody who is acquainted with its antecedents and with the way
in which the provision still works. In Italy,
at least, according to almost universal judgment, the relations of husband, wife and chil-

dren with one another are notably affectionate and charming to observe.

In conjunction with this sketch of Roman marriage we may most fittingly discuss briefly the position of women.[21] In the stricter families of correct society young daughters were probably somewhat secluded from worldly life, much as convent-bred girls of the Italian aristocracy still are, but the woman of maturity, although legally under the perpetual tutelage of some man, yet actually enjoyed through her marriage more nearly the freedom of an American than the matrons of any other ancient people. As a person of dignity, practical wisdom, energy and decision of character, she deserved it. To what extent she sometimes anticipated one American interpretation of the equality of the sexes depends upon the truthfulness of the well-known plaint of Cato the Elder: " All men rule their wives, we Romans rule all men, but our wives us." But he is credited also with that equally telltale remark: " If there had been no women in the world, the gods would still have been

[21] The relatively inferior position of the sex in contemporary Italy has been often remarked by visitors from our land, but there is a steady advance upward within recent years.

dwelling among us." Probably they did incline somewhat to harshness and to master-
fulness, true to George Eliot's reply to a
criticism of her sex: "God made them so to
match the men."

In any case we must not judge the matron
of the best periods by sporadic exceptions to
decency, although these were becoming more
and more common as the Republic came to
its end. Family life originally was simple,
pure and well-disciplined. She whom we
think of as truly Roman was mistress of the
house and addressed as such by everybody in
it, whether free or slave. Nor was she like
a Greek lady confined to a woman's quarters.[22] With her husband's knowledge she
was at liberty to walk abroad in the city, attended by her own servants. Religious
services claimed her presence outside as well
as inside the house. The theater and public
games were open to her. Our "mothers'
meetings" had their ancient prototype. A Roman matron had even the dubious privileges

[22] Of course, in such particulars the Hellenized south
of Italy must have been very different from the capital.
For various reasons Sicilian women are now narrowly
restricted in their lives. This is true of them even as
immigrants in the Italian quarters of American cities.

of testifying like a man in a court of law and, if a person of rank, of receiving like him a funeral eulogy when no longer able to profit by either praise or blame. In the home her virtue was that of the Biblical woman who " seeketh wool and flax and worketh willingly with her hands. She layeth her hands to the spindle and her hands hold the distaff." To know just what sort of loom she used for weaving, the curious need only peer into any one of several doorways in any mountain village of Italy and see it unchanged and so appreciate at least one of her ·virtues, patience, the one which now tops the list in Italy. On the other hand, such work as washing and cooking was denied her, no matter how much she might yearn for housewifely distinction in it. These were the menial tasks of slavery and of the helpless poor. Supervision was her chief duty, although, as we shall see, she might devote personal care and instruction to her children. The sight of a mother with her baby in her arms was a special delight to the Italian eye long before the first Madonna and Bambino were painted.

Among the Romans a wife received visits from relatives. Her husband's friends were hers, and, unlike her Greek sisters, she was conceded a place among the guests at table. With him she went to dinner parties. To be sure, in the " good old days " wine was not her portion, and we hear of a gracious provision that male relatives might kiss a woman to make sure that the strength of her breath was due rather to a favorite vegetable than to the fruit of the vine. However, all the other pleasures of mixed society were open to her. She even had her special festival on the first of March, when, just as on her birthday, members of the household and her friends brought her gifts and good wishes. At all times her husband would seek her counsel on family affairs. All this, if he were a good husband and she a good wife, and it is only with such, of course, that we care to deal here.

Under the free form of marriage that widely obtained under the Empire she often had the disposal of so much wealth of her own as gave her great power. No woman in any age could be courted more than some of these imperial dames. The reader must find his detailed account of all this elsewhere, a masculine picture, of course, of female frailty. Therein he will learn how with increasing legal emancipation, even sumptuary laws could not curb woman's passion for jewelry and rich raiment (the Italian propensity *far figura* is no new phenomenon);[23] how, neglecting the ancestral faith, she ran more and more after strange gods, not to speak of astrologers and fortune tellers (who never seem to be misogynists in any age!); how she meddled with man's prerogative of politics, and often as an intriguer; how she dared to acquire accomplishments, dancing more gracefully than was seemly for a reputable woman, aye even lapsed into art and literature and the seamy side of theatrical life, and began to regard marriage as only an inevitable preliminary to divorce. But these were largely women of the capital, women of the fast set, the sort who still figure in such newspapers and society sheets as print all the news that isn't fit to print, and it is only a person who believes in the time-honored (or -disgraced) double standard of morals for the sexes who will not readily admit that sexually at least men were in all periods the worse half

[23] Travellers often comment on the Italian practice of "keeping up appearances at any cost." There is a certain love of show in both sexes that accounts for much that is pleasing to the eye of an observer and is a challenge to his sense of humor.

of Roman society. The familiar sepulchral
abbreviation S. V. Q. (sine ulla querela) im-
plying a married life passed without quarreling
was probably no oftener a lie than some of
our own tombstone advertisements of virtue.

V. BIRTH AND CHILDHOOD

ONE of the most serious decisions that the *paterfamilias* had to make was at the birth of a son or daughter. The infant was laid at his feet [24] and if he wished to acknowledge it as his and provide for its uprearing, he raised it in his arms. If he refused, a servant would expose it in some public place [25] to die, or, if such were its luck, to be found by some wayfarer, who might cherish it as a child of his own or, should such be his will, bring it up to a life of slavery, professional mendicancy or vice. Such exposure of infants to die, while common enough in Greece in the Hellenistic period, seems to have been rarely, if ever, practised by the Romans until the first century of our era in

[24] The original reason why a newborn child was laid upon the earth, as he still is in some parts of Italy (Amalfi, the Abruzzi and Sicily), is forever disputable.

[25] The shelf at the door of the Ospedale di San Spirito in Rome for the deposit of undesired babies perpetuates, it would seem, an ancient opportunity of a similar sort offered by the *columna lactaria*, Paulus-Festus, Ed. of Lindsay, p. 105, 13. There used to be a similar arrangement at the Casa dei Trovatelli in Naples.

the case of a healthy child. On the other hand, an incurable cripple or an imbecile was drowned at once in accordance with convictions that would actuate some of our own physicians to do the same, did law and public opinion still permit. Even the mutilation [26] of foundlings (such as we read about in Victor Hugo's *L'Homme Qui Rit*) to increase their value as beggars with a compassionate public has ancient parallels. A female infant was less welcome than a male, even as now in poverty-stricken parts of Sicily the birth of a girl may be made known by a sign of mourning on the door. An ancient dreambook suggests one reason, in setting forth that to dream of a daughter is worse than to dream of a son since she implies a dowry and is a sort of creditor. In general, however, babies of either sex would be spared, reared and loved as Nature intended them to be. The wreath on the door where a birth had occurred stood for real joy as often surely as crape betokens sincere sorrow in a home of bereavement today. The purposed childlessness of some of the city rich under the early Empire

[26] Marquardt, *Das Privatleben der Römer*, I, p. 83, ascribes the practice to modern Italy.

for the sake of the attentions of legacy hunters was an anomalous phenomenon in striking contrast to the philo-progenitiveness — no smaller word could express it — that is so noticeable in Italy today. Even in cases where the newcomer was exposed, maternal love might insure its ultimate prosperity by putting with it some trinket or piece of jewelry which would later lead to its identification [27] and restoration perhaps to a respectable position. So at any rate the plots of Graeco-Roman comedies would lead us to believe.

Doting, ever fondling, indulgent parents are the rule in present-day Italy. They can spoil children with as much skill as any American can and are no strangers to the nursery maxim: "If at first you don't succeed, cry, cry again." Their Roman ancestors, on the contrary, at least started with a stern parental discipline. This was tempered, to be sure, by a solicitude about the safety of the baby that among our contemporaries must find its

[27] This might prevent in the nick of time the consummation of an incestuous marriage, as both pagan and Christian writers recognized. In recent times, mothers, resorting to the " *ruota* " of an Italian hospital for foundlings, have sometimes suspended from the baby's neck a token of identity known only to themselves, cf. R. Kleinpaul, *Römische Lebens- und Landschaftsbilder*, pp. 150 ff.

parallel only in homes of uncommon worry. Thus we learn that almost every conceivable activity of the child, nursing, crying, learning to stand, walk and talk, was under the tutelage of a separate deity whose good will had to be propitiated.

On the ninth day of life a boy received his *praenomen* at a special ceremony. For some reason or other which feminists may conjecture, only eight days were necessary to conclude the naming of a girl.[28] In each case the day was celebrated with a sacrifice, the burning of incense, and a lustration with water that at least suggests our rite of baptism. There was a general jollification among friends and relatives who came to congratulate the parents and to join the household in presenting the baby with its first gifts.

Birth, marriage and death were the three points in the career of man when superstitious fears reached their acme; for at these times evil spirits have ever been deemed to reach their maximum of maleficent industry. Ac-

[28] In modern Rome the baptism of a girl baby is of less importance than that of a boy, according to W. W. Story, *Roba di Roma,* 6th. Ed., I, p. 486. For the eight-day period observed in Venice see W. D. Howells, *Venetian Life,* 2nd. Ed., p. 321.

cordingly, the father early hung round his child's neck a capsule, the prototype of our lockets, containing an amulet that protected his helplessness against the evil eye and all forms of sorcery. The *bulla,* as it was called, came in the first instance from Etruria, and its material long betokened the social status of the wearer, but eventually every free-born baby displayed one of gold. The girl discarded hers on the eve of her wedding; the boy when he donned the toga of manhood for the first time. This corresponded in a way to the time when American youngsters bashfully assume the dignity of long trousers. The wearing of the *bulla,* with an amulet or some magic formula inside and sometimes inscribed with its owner's name, reminds one of the use of similar objects throughout Italy and, of course, in many parts of the world today. In particular the Italians of the south suspend by a string from the neck a small leather or cloth scapular containing a representation of the Madonna or of a saint or merely the name of such a heavenly warder. It goes by the name of *abitino* or *devozione* and works just as well as any phylactery of the ancients.

To the honor of Rome in its prime be it

said that children, as a rule, were nursed by their own mothers except in cases where the use of a wet-nurse was unavoidable. Indeed, Roman matrons in general gave their boys and girls their personal attention, although naturally they had the assistance of competent slaves who would perform the actual bathing and dressing. When we read of a preliminary chewing of baby's food by the nurse, and of an infantile diet of honey and butter,[29] we are somewhat fortified against the shocks of seeing what a *contadina* can do to her baby's stomach now without causing its immediate death. Among the peasants an infant that has never tasted wine, coffee or raw sausage has been indeed neglected.

Greek and Roman philosophers comment upon man's ill-omened cry at birth and his inability to laugh until the fortieth day thereafter; but in general infancy and childhood had none of the importance that they now have in literature and biography, so that scant information is available for our sketch. Such pictures as, for instance, that which Catullus gives us of an infant Torquatus or

[29] Upon its modern use consult A. De Gubernatis, *Storia Comparata degli Usi Natalizi in Italia e presso gli Altri Popoli Indo-Europei*, pp. 131 ff.

another of less celebrity in Statius' *Silvae* have
to be supplemented by the loveliness of certain
representations in sculpture, *e.g.,* the children
of the *Ara Pacis* reliefs. We know, however,
that the baby had his lullabys to put him to
sleep in a rocking cradle, his rhymes and stories to keep him happy while awake, and, as he
grew older, threats of ogres to make him obe-
dient. The bugaboo Lamia was quite as terri-
fying as La Befana can be now — she is not
altogether a female Santa Claus — and the
were-wolf of Petronius' day is the *lupo man-
naro* of Italian folklore and superstition. The
child went out to ride in a diminutive litter.
To start him right in his one foreign language,
a Greek was assigned very early to care for
him, so that the boy of position was likely
to grow up a bilinguist.

While the sudden transplanting of a modern man or woman into a social gathering of
ancients, even without the barrier of language,
or vice versa that of a Roman into one of
our own would result in a certain amount of
awkward embarrassment for all concerned,
the introduction of their young children would
create no such situation. Five year old
Gaius would soon feel at home with his mod-

ern mates, not only because children lack many of the social inhibitions of their elders but because so many of the simpler playthings [30] would be the same that you can find in any of the toy-booths erected for Saint Joseph's Day or for Befana's purchases for the Eve of Epiphany. One of the first that a Roman baby played with was a string of various tiny figures made into a necklace serviceable in teething. Representations of axes, swords, crescents, scissors, harpoons, etc., not only amused their possessor by their rattling but some of them also served as prophylactics against the witchcraft of the envious or hostile.

But girl babies soon graduated from these baubles to the superior joys of dolls (often articulated, though never alas! like modern creations articulate) and of the miniature equipment of doll life that we still find in the nursery. The mention of mice harnessed to a toy cart would suggest, however, a different species of nursery maid from that which may nowadays mismanage children. The pair of

[30] The evidence is strong that Rome was as indebted to Greece for its implements of play as the United States was to Germany until the Great War brought even Santa Claus under suspicion of pro-Germanism.

wheels pushed by a long handle that Italian youngsters still use is pictured in ancient monuments repeatedly, and they knew the joy of driving a team of goats — and no doubt furiously "like the driving of Jehu, the son of Nimshi"; for mercifulness has never been a birthright in the southlands of Europe. Their tops were spun in the normal European way of today by lashing with a whip and not by the mere pulling of a string. Hoops, on the other hand, were bowled along as in our streets, but a jingle of metal attachments served as the warning to get out of its way which American children prefer to shout — a degeneracy in manners shall we say! Seesaw was an amusement common to both the Greeks and Romans. Pompeian wall-paintings also prove the use of stilts. While no game with bat or racket was played, children put a ball to most other possible uses from feminine tosses of the soft, colored variety to the vigorous batting of handballs against a wall, and their elders at any rate practised a bowling game that anticipated the play at *boccia* which now amuses all ages.

A surprising number of group games that

still entertain youth originated in a forgotten past. Roman children were already enjoying Hide and Seek, Blind Man's Buff, Playing Soldiers, Odd and Even. In tossing pennies they had to shout "heads or ships" instead of "heads or tails," because such were figured on the obverse and reverse of their Republican bronze coins. Girls played with astragals as jackstones. These were the pastern bones of cloven-footed animals, such as sheep and goats, and are a common plaything around the Mediterranean still. For marbles they used and continue to use round pebbles or nuts, almonds in August, but, better still, hazel nuts at Christmas. An Italian game that a Roman boy could join without instruction consists in pyramiding four nuts to make a castle which is to be demolished by the casting of a fifth. Even board-games like chess, checkers and backgammon have ancient precursors that were highly popular, as wall-paintings and terra-cotta figures along with allusions in literature attest.

Somewhere between fourteen and seventeen, as a rule, boys exchanged their robe of boyhood at a special social and religious function which congratulating friends and relatives would attend. It was a glad day for the youth, who now dispensed with the supervision of his *paedagogus*, his inseparable shadow, and went his own ways. It was a proud day for the father, whose visit to the Forum with a son now able to share in all the activities of Roman citizenship meant a shower of felicitations from all his business or professional acquaintances. But before we take the fledgling any further in his flight, we must consider briefly how he had been educated.

Roman education is honored as it deserves in this series with a special treatise, so that we need not deal in detail with either its form or its spirit. Until the time of the Empire, the government left the moral and intellectual training of future citizens wholly to their parents and to private schooling. To this day in Italy, there is no such state control as there is with us. Education was without any standardization, neglected the masses, and fortified the natural conservatism of the privileged few who enjoyed it. Practical wisdom was the goal; for the Romans were nothing if they were not utilitarian to the last degree. Civic usefulness, intense patriotism, ready obedience to authority,[31] willingness to work with others, respect for ancestral tradition, scrupulous observance of religious rites, these were the lessons emphasized in home and school. Until the Romans became strongly Hellenized, discipline rather than culture was the aim, and dutifulness (*pietas*) in all relationships of life might be termed the pinnacle of their house of virtues. Parents then recognized how much more personal example counted than any delegated teaching or bookish precept. Accordingly, the old-fashioned father would himself instruct his boys in the physical training and manly sports that he believed produced not only a skilled soldier but a good citizen. The Roman attitude towards athletics deserves indeed some special notice.

While Rome did not continue for us the noble example that Greece set in her prime by pursuing sport for sport's sake and shunning the spirit of professionalism, yet she did transmit some of the Hellenic appreciation of physical training as a preservative of health. It was

[31] The attitude of the Italian masses today towards rules and regulations cannot be accounted one of the survivals from Roman times. Prohibitive placards merely give an extra zest to the pleasures of indulgence.

a Roman who said *mens sana in corpore sano*.
Moreover, they realized, as Americans only
recently have begun to do, that exercise cannot wisely be confined to youth alone. Rome's
greatest statesmen enjoyed games of ball with
the same propriety that ours may now play
golf on the last six days of the week, although
they sometimes had their thoughts, I fear,
much more upon the bodily advantage to be
derived from it than upon any fun. In fact,
our great group-contests of baseball, football,
lacrosse and cricket lacked an ancient
counterpart,[32] and Rome had no such thing
as a national game. In the time of her spread-
ing conquests, interest turned rather to that
individual efficiency that militarism demands.
A youth must run and jump, and learn to
swim and ride and wrestle and fence, because
only so could he hope to overcome his foe, or,
if need be, live to fight another day by making a speedy escape. At the Capital, the
Campus Martius, a great level stretch in a
fold of the river Tiber, drew throngs of men
and boys for a swim, the foot race, the long

[32] The only possible exception known to the writer,
the contests of the σφαιρεῖς at Sparta, is by no means
a sure one.

or high jump, boxing, wrestling, throwing the discus or javelin, or some variety of ball playing. But no Roman maid or matron had the Spartan privilege of competitive sports in such a place. Indeed, the mere sight of a game of basket ball between teams of girls would have struck Cicero as a portent to be expiated by the sacrifice of a black sheep. Still even now the health of an Italian girl cannot be attributed to any such life of sport as is the joy of her sex in Anglo-Saxon communities. On the other hand, within recent years her brothers have certainly taken up athletics with an almost American ardor, although, curiously enough, independently of their school life.

A Roman wife instructed both her sons and daughters in the preliminaries to school learning. Since most of the clothing even in the noblest families was likely to be home-made — Augustus dared to wear in public the creations of three generations of his women folk — girls were taught to weave, spin and sew, and no higher tribute could be paid at death to a matron than that she stayed by the house and attended to her wool. This remains the prevalent view of woman's place in most of southern Europe, where the extra-mural activities and superactivities of the sex in America are regarded as unseemly, if not unfeminine. *Eppur si muove!*

The daughter in a Roman house might have the prototype of a Spanish *duenna* as her escort and governess, but sometimes the slave was a male and not necessarily superannuated. She had to be equipped to act as mistress of a husband's home and household long before the normal age for matrimony in the United States, and it was fortunate for those whose social rank did not limit them to private tutors at home, as so many girls in Italy are now restricted, that they secured at least a slight insight into masculine ways through co-education in the primary school. As a matter of fact, such was the disparity common between the ages of wife and husband that the latter often began his married life as a sort of father and school teacher as well as spouse to his mate.

As for the Roman boy, if his special guardian slave, the *paedagogus*, had been carefully chosen, he would learn much from him to the betterment of mind, manners and morals, but it would be from personal observation and imitation [33] of his father that he would derive his knowledge of a business or profession. Thus, he listened as his parent advised a client, delivered a speech, or scintillated in prandial repartee; he watched him and often served him as his acolyte as he performed a sacrifice. For a period, too, sons enjoyed the privilege of attending meetings of the senate with their fathers; but this had to be stopped, we are told, because mothers tried to make their boys divulge the secrets of the sessions — one of the few ancient records of that curiosity which is now so noticeable to the foreigner in the Italian of both sexes.

The discipline of the schools was harsh; [34] the noise unendurable for neighbors, the prizes of a rare or pretty book or the like rarely conferred, the punishments more memorable than their lessons in the " three R's," the pay of the teacher generally so low as to be an acceptable model for retrograde communities in all subsequent history.

[33] It is from Italy that we have imported a revival of this apprentice type of education in the Montessori method.

[34] The Roman school boy had reason to believe that Prometheus stole fire from heaven in the hollow of a cane, if caught putting oil in his eyes to incapacitate them for study or chewing cumin to induce the pallor of illness.

After the elementary schools those of grammar and of rhetoric acquainted the pupil with the literary culture both of Greece and of the fatherland. Homer, Cicero, Virgil and Horace were already text books eighteen centuries and more ago. Thus he reached the mental maturity when he might be sent abroad for what corresponds somewhat to our college education. In Greece Romans of the upper class amended their relative racial boorishness by contact with a people that, however much it had deteriorated, was yet superior to the Latin in taste and learning. Athens was a university town. There philosophy and rhetoric might be studied under the most famous professors, but there were besides other important centers of learning further away, such as Alexandria, Rhodes and the great cities of Asia Minor, where Roman youths could broaden their minds by contact with strange peoples and by the contemplation of masterpieces of art. Incidentally they gained a final polish for their Greek, which with their own tongue constituted the world languages of antiquity.

The young aristocrat who aspired to be a statesman and possessed political influence

often went abroad on the staff of some pro-
vincial governor, thereby acquiring, along with
a certain amount of tainted money, if he had
luck and few scruples, an experience of the
world that served him in good stead when
he himself became an administrator.

While farming and stock raising occupied
most of the Romans during the early history
of their country and they never ceased to be
proper vocations for even the most patrician,
during the closing years of the Republic it
was rather the army or public oratory and the
bar [35] that would claim a high-born youth when
he reached the age of manhood. If he chose
the former which was less likely under the
Empire, some general would take him under
his personal charge and training, if the latter,
some distinguished advocate and jurist. The
money-making of knight and senator (the
latter largely through agents, since he was not
supposed to do any business personally) in
a city where Mammon ought to have been
officially recognized as almost a super-god
among her deities, does not belong to our
descriptions here. A boy of the middle or

[35] Class feelings, or, if you will, prejudices largely
account for the existence, and too often the bare existence of a superfluity of lawyers in Italy today.

lower classes passed, of course, from school into the business of life with no social stir; but him we must ignore as any old Roman patrician would have done, though for other reasons.

Before we drop our review of the members of a Roman household we must not forget their pets. The evidence of both literature and the monuments would lead us to believe that the ancients lived in domestic intimacy with their animals. Even Italians who are much above the lowest classes still do. One need not resort to an inn in some remote and primitive village, if he would have pigeons flutter down to the table where he eats, hens roost on the foot-board of his bed, and dogs and cats brush against his legs in the rôle of lover or of mendicant, no matter where he sits. If the tavern cat has lost the tip of its tail, refer it not to accident but to a widespread superstition that all the evil of the animal being localized in its end, this should be bitten off as early as possible. Still this hypothetical evil did not appear in ancient Rome until the imperial age, when Egypt began to export there some of her tame cats. Previously the weasel had to play her part

as mice-exterminator, but surely less agree-
ably. Romans kept other creatures domesticated that we locate more comfortably for
ourselves in a Zoo. The snake was a protected animal in the home, not merely as an
enemy of rodents [36] but because, if a male,
it incarnated the Genius of the master and,
if a female, the Juno of the mistress, so that
the destruction of one might lead to the death
of the corresponding human being. This accounts for the story told of Tiberius Gracchus
that when he found two snakes in his bed and
was bidden by the diviners to kill one, he
chose the male that he might perish first (as
he soon did), rather than his young wife,
Cornelia, whom he dearly loved. Monkeys
had much in the columnar home to provide
them with the exercises of their native haunts,
but their escape to neighboring roofs through
the rain-hole was a nuisance.

Birds [37] were the favorite pets, ranging in
size from the diminutive sparrow — anciently a

[36] In the Philippine Islands women visitors have to
divide their antipathies between the mice and the large
snake who is domesticated to eat the mice. Similarly
in Brazil a small boa constrictor, the gibola, has to take
the place of the cat.

[37] Before the days of firearms Italy must have been
a vast aviary. Now that Nimrods patrol every rod of

[79]

bird of love and not a pest [38] — through doves
and quails to ducks and geese. The almost
universal suspension of a bird cage at the
front door in many parts of Italy is, therefore,
quite in accord with ancient practice. Talk-
ing birds were particularly popular and the
" good morning " that greeted you at a door
did not of necessity come from human lips.
The pugnacity of quails and cocks accounted
for their popularity with sporting youth.

the land, a bird who exchanges a subdued twitter for a
real song is dead.

[38] Ornithologists query the use of the term " sparrow "
for *passer*. Lesbia's pet was possibly. as Samuel Butler
(*Alps and Sanctuaries*, pp. 230–231) believed, the *passero
solitario*, a peerless singer: surely we must not think of
her *deliciae* in terms of the " English sparrow," our urban
scavenger.

VI. CLOTHING

OUR consideration of the inhabitants of a Roman house brings us next to an account of the clothes they wore. While detailed description is quite impossible here, certain generalities are in place. As one might presuppose among the descendants of a pastoral people, the universal material for their apparel was wool, until exposure to foreign seductions towards the beginning of the Empire gradually brought other stuffs into vogue. Italians still appreciate the wisdom of wearing wool even in the heat of summer, and the theory that the degeneracy of Rome was partially due to her desertion of that material would find more favor with *contadini* than with some of our closet-scholars. In any case, a certain debasement in morality can be associated with the advent from Oriental sources (verily *ex Oriente lux!*) of thin or transparent tissues [39] of silk, linen

[39] " Woven wind " was a Roman's apt characterization of such disclosive clothing. Women who have purchased at Taranto scarfs made from the silky beard of

and cotton, which Roman women came to love and even the law could not prevent men from wearing. Yet as late as the fourth century of our era raiment entirely of silk was esteemed a mad extravagance. Times have changed!

In general, however, the clothes of both sexes, when compared with the products of modern sartorial genius, seem very simple, and changes in style were then slower and slighter. The full tyranny of tailor and dressmaker had yet to be established with its terrific consumption of time and money. The hairdresser alone appears to have had that domination over both sexes that the despotism of Dame Fashion nowadays creates.

Under the Republic white and certain sombre tinges of the natural wool were the only colors in general use. Uniforms, however, had already been invented, and for the distinctions that such costumes required they used an expensive dye made from purple shell-fish. This seems to have had a color-scale ranging from a deep orange to an almost

the *lana-pesce,* the shell-fish known to science as the *pinna nobilis,* may be interested to know that the diaphanous garments of ancient dancing-girls were woven from this same product.

black purple and to have left an odor that might well be said to make the wearer of the garment " smell of money," as the vulgar put it. Our theatrical costumers could reduce their anachronisms somewhat by striping Roman senatorial robes with crimson rather than with royal purple. The imperial age brought women and to a lesser degree men a chance for that riot of color that we now expect to see among Mediterranean peoples. They began, indeed, to have the more delicate half-shades along with the pure tints.

So far as the cut of their clothing is concerned, the sexes used to dress much more alike than at the present time. Hailing a person at a distance had in fact the same uncertainties which it did recently for a brief but anxious spell when women blossomed into bloomer costumes, and as it may again, if, as seems likely, knickerbockers complete their capture of the feminine fancy.

The constriction of hats, corsets, belts, garters, stockings, boots and gloves to which we submit would excite the compassion and often the risibility of an ancient, and in his judgment might have accounted for the scant inspiration now available for the development of a Praxiteles or a Polyclitus. The outdoor life of the modern Italian and his consequent ability to endure extremes of heat and cold is a fine tradition from his forefathers. The scant apparel of the poor even in the winter months excites among foreign observers a commiseration which may be more fittingly bestowed upon other conditions. It is a matter of record that Italians in ordinary clothing have withstood the rigors of Arctic cold better than Scandinavians in heavy furs.

One of the many mythological stories that charm by their naïve wickedness sets forth that when Cronus thought to devour his own son Zeus, Rhea thwarted his cannibalism by presenting him with a stone, which he swallowed without knowing the difference. Now it is somewhat difficult to understand how even the simplicity of a Greek deity could have been fooled by such a substitution until one has actually noted with his own eyes the resemblance to an elongated pill or capsule which a baby in Greece or Italy often bears by the time he has been swaddled in a band some five inches wide and many yards in length.

The wrapping [40] may confine both arms and legs closely, so that the resulting bundle seems to be enough like a stone to be stood on end, either end, without fear of breakage, no matter how fragile the infant. As if this were not enough to fortify the baby against all dangers, nurses put inside the folds a bit of garlic [41] which might be deemed strong enough to repel even vampirical spirits. Italian infants, too young to say for themselves the avertive " *fora-fascino* " or " *benedica*," must even now wear some prophylactic against the evil eye.

By the time ancient children had escaped these swaddling clothes, they might pass into that perfect freedom of nakedness that is not rare during the summer in the more tropical

[40] Hawthorne thought that the custom might be responsible for an excess of dwarfs, and Charles Dickens for a superabundance of cripples, while W. W. Story, a much better informed observer, has a good word for the practice.

[41] It symbolizes health and strength today in both Greece and Italy. Peasants value it especially as a prophylactic against cholera. Pitré includes a *testa d'agghia* in his picture of Sicilian amulets, *Catalogo Illustrato della Mostra Etnografica Siciliana* (1892), p. 77, No. 217. Compare p. 78, No. 218, for other safeguards against magic worn by contemporary babies.

sections of Italy today. At most, their frolics would be hampered by an abbreviated tunic. Only boys and girls of well-to-do families had to suffer over their shirt on all dressy occasions a "purple" bordered gown, the so-called *toga praetexta*, a miniature of the robe that distinguished the higher magistrates. We have, therefore, in this a chance anticipation of the similarity of the short trousers that schoolboys wear to the court dress of England. The Roman girl laid aside this robe at marriage, the boy upon coming of age, replacing it by the garments of maturity, which we must now describe.

During the cold of winter a Roman who was neither an invalid nor an effeminate would wear at most one or two woolen tunics between his linen loin cloth and his *toga* or outer garment, while in summer out of doors he might, if comfort contended with convention, dispense with his shirts altogether. In the house, if heat led him to discard his *toga*, he would, of course, still wear a tunic. This was provided with a girdle and reached just below the knee. The *toga* was a white woolen robe, once scanty but finally voluminous. It was the outward badge of Roman citizenship, as significant, indeed, as the possession of the pig-tail used to be in China. It had to be worn at all social functions, as well as for all official business, even under the early Empire when unconventional people began to substitute for it, whenever they could or dared, the less cumbersome cloak or mantle form of outer garment, or even (like the tradespeople at all periods) wear nothing at all over the tunic.

No national costume now is so jealously guarded and so distinctive as the *toga* used to be. Charon could identify at sight a citizen of the greatest of all empires, no matter where he died; for, if a genuine Roman, he came to the Styx in that same garment as his shroud. The dignity of the *toga* accorded indeed with the proud assertion *Civis Romanus sum,* and it long protected its wearer quite as the Union Jack an Englishman though he were at the very ends of the earth. Should we wonder that some of our earlier sculptors,[42] when commissioned to portray an American statesman, in their despair of making him look great in coat, waistcoat and trousers, often resorted to a brazen anachronism, and put him into

[42] Nathaniel Hawthorne tells us how the sculptor Hiram Powers worried about representing Washington in breeches.

what seemed to their untutored minds to be a *toga?*

As a matter of fact, the shape of this Roman garment changed greatly from the earliest historical times, when it was worn in war as well as in peace, by women as well as by men, and perhaps as a mantle fastened by a brooch, to the classical period, when it was a robe symbolic of peace and among women was worn only by the harlot. Its precise cut and arrangement still cause the experts to wrangle in the presence of the ancient statues, although in general we know how it was put on.

Those who wonder how the wearer could have managed his hands and arms need only observe the graceful Italian officers in the ample military capes which they don in winter. The truth is, the Roman gentleman had to know how to wear it and needed his valet's skill to lay the folds and creases aright. The style, cut and set of his *toga* would indeed differentiate the upstart vulgarian from a man of birth and breeding quite as mercilessly as some modern sartorial tests.

In contrast with the effeminacy of loose and somewhat flowing robes, trousers seem to us

Occidentals a thoroughly civilized and manly garb, but the classic peoples held a contrary opinion. The Greeks deemed them fit for only the barbarians [43] to wear, and, although Roman soldiers did resort to their comfort and convenience during winter campaigns abroad, it was long before polite society in the capital would condescend to put them on; but ultimately we find an emperor, Alexander Severus, wearing white ones, superseding an earlier style which had required scarlet, and we can only guess whether imitative courtiers followed suit. Stockings [44] also and any sort of gloves or neckwear were at Rome the privilege of age or invalidism rather than of manhood in its prime. Even long sleeves on a tunic were accounted effeminate.

Of the other garments that more and more displaced the *toga* for ordinary undress occasions, the cloaks, mantles, and ponchos with their hoods, space forbids an account. The peasants and shepherds would wear goat skins

[43] If we may trust the ancient monuments, the type still worn in Persia and among the Cossacks perpetuates the fashions prevalent there two thousand years ago.

[44] Shepherds and huntsmen, however, might wear the leggings or puttees which the experience of modern warfare has made so popular.

and sheep skins, even as they still do. One has to see some of the shepherds in wild and remote districts to understand what " a wolf in sheep's clothing " really means. Even hats [45] in the period with which we are dealing were used by gentlemen ordinarily only on a journey or sometimes in a wide-brimmed style in the open theater. Laborers, however, wore them, and if their use had been general among all classes, we might have missed some of the countless references to eye troubles which seem to have been almost an endemic ailment.

The rules of religion prescribed that a person sacrificing should have his head covered. Accordingly we find the *toga* represented as pulled up over the crown, much as Italian women raise their shawls upon entering a church or, in the lack of one, place a handkerchief on their hair. The way in which both sexes used to protect themselves against a cold wind or sudden downpour is nowadays demonstrated even by the men in Sicily, who use a shawl for a head and shoulder wrap.

[45] Our liberty-cap (compare the French *bonnet-rouge*) is the modern representative of the *pilleus,* the cap which the Roman slave donned at his manumission to symbolize his freedom and which everybody wore at the *Saturnalia* as the token of liberty.

[90]

In the house both sexes wore slippers and sandals, out of doors boots and shoes, nor was there anything to distinguish between those of men and women except perhaps that the latter possessed those of better quality and finish. Men did have, to be sure, shoes which declared by the differences of color, ornament or fastenings the social or official position of the owner. Their use of straps or thongs, encircling the ankle and lower calf, would now be best illustrated by the footgear of very humble rustics, such as the *ciocie* worn so largely in one region of Italy that it is often called *La Ciociaria*. The use of wood for shoes and sandals is also perpetuated in Italy as well as exemplified in the French *sabots* and the English clogs.

Roman women wore an inner tunic so much like that of the mèn that we can imagine an interchange to have been at times a family convenience, at times a provocative of trouble. They supported the bosom by a breast band of soft leather, but wore nothing that can properly be likened to a laced and boned corset [46] either beneath the dress or, as often

[46] This is sound as a general statement, although Sig. Castellani once showed me figurines in his collection

among Italian peasants of today, outside of it. They resorted to gentler means to improve the endowments of nature, but were already engaged in the fight against that obesity which is still the chief menace to Italian beauty.

An upper tunic, the *stola,* the ultimate forbear of the ecclesiastical stole, was the distinctive apparel of a Roman woman and safeguarded her in public much as the dress of a Salvation Army lass does its wearer. It usually had short sleeves, if the undershirt lacked them, was girdled and reached to the feet, where in the case of the matrons [47] there was a border to distinguish them from the unmarried girl.

As an outer garment women wore a rectangular shawl, white, black or colored, which was commonly draped much as the *toga* of the men in its simpler form. Anciently men were as badly off for pockets as the women were. Both had to trust to the folds of their

which pictured women adjusting what was amazingly similar to a modern corset, nor must we forget that, long before Rome was thought of, certain Cretan pictures apparently of tight-laced men suggest the possibility that our *Urvater* Adam may have taught Eve the practice.

[47] Wives who had borne children were privileged to wear a special type of stole in honor of their motherhood.

garments. There was, however, more excuse for this inconvenience in the days when a slave was at hand to carry anything that can now be forced into the bulging pockets of an uxorious husband.

Long hair and beard distinguished the early Romans, but Hellenistic influence through Sicily finally induced them to shave. A sight of the bronze razors which the ancients used wins credit for the tradition that the first in Rome to shave habitually was a hero, Scipio Africanus the Elder. In the early imperial period a man's first beard-cutting was often made a festal occasion, and the clippings were dedicated to some god. Except for philosophers, who had to look wise, and certain youths, like the dandies of Cicero's day, who had to "look smart," and men of the lower classes, who had no right to care how they looked anyway, smooth faces continued in style down to the reign of Hadrian whose need to hide certain facial blemishes brought beards into vogue again for a long time.

The hair was worn short, except when mourning prescribed a total disuse of the scissors even for the beard. Men, so-called, even practised depilation. Curling the hair also was sometimes in fashion for men who affected elegance, perfuming it always for those who could afford the cost. The stronger the odor, the longer the purse.

Since women of old were limited in the amount of individuality and artistry that they could show in the fashioning of clothes, they had to turn such talents as were their legacy from Eve — or was it Pyrrha? — to varying their ornaments of jewelry and the dressing of their hair. Consequently there is almost no arrangement of natural or of artificial locks that our last century of ingenuity has invented that the patience of the archaeologist cannot match with some ancient crown of glory or of horror, unless perchance we must except a coiffure recently popular among Neapolitans; they fluff up their rather crinkly hair behind so that it stands erect precisely as if the back part of the head had been scared by some canine adversary. But really the marvel of even this is surpassed by the creations of court ladies under the early Empire, as we know them from surviving monuments and from coins. No pen of mere man can describe their towering magnificence (*e.g.*, tier upon tier of perfectly symmetrical curls), their complicated convolutions, their elaborate plaits, their rhythmic undulations, least of all the hidden amplifiers and supports that constituted their true inwardness. Fortunately styles for maid and matron were not the same. The former displayed something simpler, for instance one instead of two of the fillets that only the Roman citizen could wear.

In contemporary Italy, women who belong to the so-called peasant class are conveniently identified by the fact that they go bareheaded [48] except, of course, when labor under a tropical sun leads them to top their hair with many thicknesses of folded toweling, *tovaglie*. In this they follow a wholesome precedent set by the humble of antiquity. On the other hand, a married woman of social position was expected to have her head covered in the public streets, and, at one time, failure to observe this requirement might even cause a divorce. A scarf or mantle was sufficient veiling. Romans knew nothing like our feminine hats and bonnets. Verily the

---

[48] In the Italian quarter in New York one of the Cinisi may say scornfully: "Look at that *villana*. In the old country she used to carry baskets of tomatoes on her head and now she carries a hat on it." Park and Miller, *Old World Traits Transplanted*, p. 147.

sight of some of these would lay the ghost of an ancient lady as quickly as that of a cigarette in the mouth of either sex would lay the ghost of a man. But there are today in Italy secluded villagers who have never seen a hat on a lady's head. As an extra protection against the severities of nature ribbed parasols that opened and shut were already available. Fans, too, were much in use.

The women of ancient Italy, though as a rule blessed, as they still are, with beautiful heads of luxuriant, dark, glossy hair, which has a natural inclination to behave prettily in curls and wavy tresses, used to envy their own slaves of northern origin the possession of locks of lighter hue. What is more, there were those who would shave their own hair in order to wear wigs of imported red or yellow, or, in default of these, they would apply a chemical treatment that would make them at first blonde but presently alas! bald. Even the tonics, oils and unguents with which they coaxed lustre into healthy hair or sought to thicken it could not repair this damage, as Ovid is rude enough to tell one of his sweethearts in misfortune. The admiration for light-haired children is still strong in swarthy

Italy. For instance, at Caltagirone at Christmas they have to select some three year old to play the rôle of the Bambino Jesus and with singular inappropriateness they regularly choose a blonde.

It would be ungallant, however, for a man even of our period to dwell in detail upon all the mysteries of a Roman boudoir as literature and archaeology ruthlessly reveal them to those who are curious of such things. The rouge is yet to be seen in the toilet-pyx. Pompeii discloses powder boxes of her ancient belles. We read of women who dared not expose their complexions to the sun lest the enamel melt, their curls to the rain lest stringy locks should result, nor even cough lest they lose their teeth. Beauty patches were gummed on marble brows sixteen centuries before the days of Queen Anne. Hairs, badly disposed from the point of view of comeliness, would be removed with tweezers or a depilatory, those absent altogether but needed badly could be painted in with a dark pomade. As a rule, however, incipient whiskers and adolescent mustaches were more likely to mar the southern woman than baldness either sex. But they stopped at nothing in their personal embellishment. Even a blue vein on a whitened brow might not withstand the effects of water, and rosy lips were not all that they sometimes seemed.

For the most part, however, cosmetics were more largely used by the women of Greece because of their rather harem-like existence. To the credit of contemporary Italy be it said that natural complexions are much more in evidence there than in the United States, where even negroes powder and where face-paint is no longer as sure an index of indelicacy as it used to be. Of course, Roman men were in this race of vanity and folly also, but shame makes us forbear to tell just how close they ran their rivals.

It is pleasanter to dwell upon the passion of both sexes for jewelry. There was no point of attachment to the person that was not in use except that they neglected to pierce the nose and lips. Women wore finger rings, bracelets, armlets, necklaces, breast-chains, earrings, brooches, jewelled buttons, ornamental hairpins, hair nets of solid gold, and even anklets.[49] The passion still persists in

[49] If these last were practically a monopoly of freed-women, it was partly no doubt because the matron's

Italy, where a baby needs be but a few weeks old to enjoy its first earrings, while its peasant mother may have pendants so long and heavy that their removal is a proper preliminary (as in Sicily) to any physical try-out with a neighbor. Massiveness and weight were characteristic of ancient Roman jewelry also. There was considerable etiquette in its use; for instance, in time of national sorrow, one should substitute iron finger rings for gold. For fastening garments, both sexes must have used *fibulae* in no small number during the course of a lifetime; for the quantity that has been found is past calculation. While many varieties of gems were in fashion for jewelry, no cut stone had the value of a pearl in Roman estimation; to secure primacy the diamond had to await an age when workmen could give it brilliant facets.

Men were denied the esthetic opportunities that shirts, cuffs, neckties and watches afford their descendants, but they could display their taste in the choice of rings. One with a signet was a real necessity, since sealing was a usual protection not only for documents

stole was so long as to make the display of such circlets difficult.

but for money-caskets, food-closets, store-rooms and the like. To this day, a bit of sealing wax is a surer safeguard against robbery than most locks, as the traveller, experienced in Italy, well knows.

VII. GODS

THE house had other inhabitants, not yet discussed, whom its occupants never forgot, namely the gods. It was their presence that gave the Roman dwelling that special sanctity and those who lived in it the peculiar sentiment which we associate with the word home — a new idea in the ancient world, a novelty still in much of ours. The fire-spirit Vesta had dwelt in the hearth ever since there was a flame to kindle. The first storing of a food supply by the provident brought into being the Penates or divinities of the larder. The family would usually have its own particular selection from among the higher gods also, whom it revered much as the Latin races their patron saints of home and city. The master of the house had his special tutelary deity, a sort of other self, the so-called Genius, the procreative spirit responsible for family continuity, while his consort had a corresponding divine being in her Juno. Under the influence of Greek anthropomorphism, the Genius is often imaged as a *toga*-clad figure holding a cornucopia. Further, at Pompeii, at any rate, both of these spirits may be symbolized by snakes painted on the wall, a bearded male for the Genius, a female for the Juno. They used to represent them in places they wished to keep undefiled, even as Italians still paint the Christian cross on house walls for the same purpose but with small effect. Other protecting divinities, the Lares (whether in origin local spirits, or those of the family ancestors, or merely general spirits, nobody really knows), abode with their human friends in the likeness of youths, clad in short tunics, who are dancing while pouring a libation, as it were, in their own honor. Nor must we omit to mention the divine powers that religious fear and fancy associated with almost every action of daily existence without ever visualizing them as painted or sculptured figures. Home and land were as full of them as a properly populated Irish village teems with fairies.

For the worship of all these spiritual beings [50] we find provision made not only by shrines and altars in various parts of the dwelling but also in more pretentious homes

[50] The Roman *dii cubiculares,* gods of the bedroom, make us think of the saints and the Madonna and

by a separate chapel or oratory, as we might call it, for their special use. Since the relations of the pagans with divinity were primarily of a business nature, an interchange of a *quid pro quo*, the two being as much out of proportion to each other as shrewdness could contrive, we find them making vows of this or that object in return for the god's boon. These votives would then, on the receipt of the blessing [51] asked for, be consigned to some place where the god was localized *e.g.*, the private shrine or a public temple.[52] The offerings that have come down to us are commonly of the same sort that are used in Christian churches all over the peninsula now, notable being representations of every part of the human anatomy that can be impaired and cured, and also pictures of all sorts of disasters from

Bambino that look down benignly from niche or frame upon countless Italian beds. Moreover, even the most sacred images suffer maltreatment, just as of old, when disappointment in the divine protector has changed pious faith to impious rage.

[51] The obligation to pay was as solemn then as now; compare H. F. Jones, *Castellinaria*, pp. 238 and 255.

[52] Where there are famous healing shrines as *e.g.* in S. Agostino in Rome, nearby shops supply the *ex-votos* quite as they did two millennia ago near the bridge that led to the Temple of Aesculapius on the island in the Tiber which served as a sort of hospital.

which piety effects a rescue. The Madonna receives now the same kind of art that Isis got in the days of Juvenal.

If it was hard for the first Christians in their proselyting to make clear to many of the heathen such tenets as that prayer with no material accompaniment was a fit offering to a spiritual being, it is probably no less difficult for us to realize all the effects upon a household of bloody sacrifices inuring increasingly even the most sensitive to scenes of suffering. But even modern children, if reared in a slaughter-house, might not be squeamish about the gore of a gladiatorial arena.

However much the public state religion of Rome may have suffered by the close of the Republic, we have reason to believe that household worship was still vigorous and sincere. This warmer, more emotional type of faith which finds outlet today all over Italy in the ever-burning taper, or (thanks to the triumph of material progress over what is poetical in life!) in the tiny electric light before the Madonna's picture in shop and home, may well have been much commoner than were the scepticism and scorn of the educated for all the fatuities of polytheism.

There would seem to have been many pious souls who offered daily prayer and sacrifice in the morning as well as paid the due rites at the evening meal, when in fact the statuettes of the Lares might be set on the dining-table as a reminder of heaven's part in the procuring of its blessings. Then, too, important events in the family, such as birthdays, required religious observances quite as much as the festal days of the state calendar, nor would these always mean merely such tributes as burning incense [53] or a libation of wine, but they might involve the slaying of a pig. This brought a pleasing change in the menu of the family, since deity generously shared the best of the beast with his worshippers.

In all these sacrificial performances ritualistic accuracy was the main thing. Similarly in Sicilian witchcraft today an incantation must be letter-perfect or else it will not work. A single slip will require the repetition of the whole spell. From all this it may appear how deeply Roman religion could affect domestic life and that, too, for seven days out of every week.

[53] Although no longer needed to neutralize the odor of burnt or bloody sacrifices, incense has never lost in Italy its importance as a symbol or vehicle of prayer.

VIII. DAILY LIFE

THE usual routine of a Roman gentleman's day at the capital is known to us from literature. The possible modifications of it due to the tastes or status of the individual, to his place of residence, or to the season of the year cannot be detailed here. Among the Romans an hour was one twelfth of the period between sunrise and sunset, so that its length was constantly changing. Moreover, the lack of our instruments of precision made living according to any strict schedule difficult. Sensitiveness to the arrival or departure of a mere point of time is, however, even today foreign to the Italian nature.

The Roman rose in the neighborhood of sunrise. In much of Italy a tourist is ready to do so now, unless he be hard of hearing. In some of the hill-towns one might conclude that the poorer inhabitants all got up at four and the richer went to bed at five. Between the two, Martial's complaints of sleep-destroying noises are verified eighteen centuries later. Old-fashioned people probably continued the custom of starting the day with sacrifice and prayer to the gods, in which the servants were expected to share as at family prayers in our own more pious past.

The first meal resembled in its lightness and brevity what we call the "continental breakfast," but, of course, there was no coffee or other hot drink to enable the early riser "to start the day right." Bread was then as at present among the poor of Italy much more truly the staff of life than it is in American homes, now that the invasion of soft cereals has relieved us of the necessity of chewing and therefore also, often, before mid-life, of our more important teeth. We have reason to believe that anciently ordinary bread [54] was hard and coarse enough to keep the teeth bright and the jaws strong. Grit from the mill-stones likened it to loaves that one must still eat in primitive sections of Italy or else go hungry. The baking itself might add a few cinders; for they used what we call a Dutch oven in which great heat is

[54] At Pompeii at any rate the practice appears to have been the same as in modern Italy to purchase the family supply at a bakeshop.

quickly generated by a fire of twigs and brush. After the ashes had been removed, the loaves were shut up inside to bake. This operation may be seen anywhere in Italy to this day. The Roman made his bread more palatable by a sprinkle of salt or by dipping it in wine, as peasants do now, or, occasionally by accompanying it with olives, raisins or a bit of cheese. Milk or a mixture of wine and honey would be the beverage of the hearty, who also sometimes added eggs to their bill of fare, especially if the breakfast were belated so as to make unnecessary a noontime meal.

Business or professional duties claimed the hours immediately following breakfast. But first of all came the *salutatio,* a morning reception which for many generations fashionable usage forced upon society, although it was as irksome to all the participants as certain functions that imperious Fashion still imposes on her unhappy slaves. He who received at such a levee as well as all the guests had to appear in the *toga* of full dress,[55] and the hurry from all quarters of the city on a

[55] " Toga-wearer," *togatus,* from its application to parasitical clients gradually degenerated from an epithet of honorable distinction to a term of contempt.

hot day put those who came on foot in a heavy
perspiration and in no good humor long before
their arrival. The humbler among them
might have to submit to indignities from
haughty, toll-taking servants posted between
the front door and their lord in the *atrium*.
Moreover, the latter sometimes needed the
service of his *nomenclator* or name-caller to
whisper some account of approaching no-
bodies so that he might not inquire politely
concerning the wife of one who was a bachelor
or concerning an infant of the childless. The
memory of this usher would owe its perfection to ever-impending penalties only less
severe than those inflicted for forgetfulness
by an African prince upon his official " re-
membrancer."

It was under the early Empire especially,
when the size of a man's following no longer
had any political significance, that the hang-
ers-on ranged through many grades of society
and included brazen sycophants, professional
legacy hunters, chronic loafers, moneyless
prodigals and the like, along with perfectly
respectable people who had been made para-
sites by the system. Of course, friends received a greeting that corresponded to their

intimacy and affection. Men kissed one another quite as freely as we see them doing it in Latin countries. The hand-kissing that is so offensive to some Americans in Italy we need not blame necessarily upon the conventional manners of the Bourbon period; the custom was prevalent enough in Rome thousands of years ago, and perhaps never died out.

Some of the morning callers would be asked to attend their host on his way down town, or perhaps be invited to dinner. In the days when the size of a man's retinue was an outward token of his standing, the lesser sort were expected to follow his litter through dust or mud. In return for their humiliating servilities, these clients received not only the rewards that pensioners often do in our age, for instance, a cast-off garment, a sum of money or influential support in time of trouble, but also a daily meal or its equivalent in money.[56] The social degradation due to the fetching away of food in a basket, received from the hands of a supercilious flunkey, and, in gen-

[56] Parallels for this may be found in modern Italy. See *Under Petraia with some saunterings*, pp. 122-123.

eral, the snobbery attaching to such relationships need no comment here.

Various duties, some of a purely social
nature, might fall to the morning hours of a
man of fashion such as visits of condolence
or congratulation, or to the bed of the sick,
canvassing to elect a friend or relative to political office in the days when electioneering
still counted for something, or, at a later age,
listening to a semi-public recitation by an
author, who then risked in return a similar
boredom as an auditor of his former host,
serving as a witness at the signing of a will,
or attendance at the inauguration of a magistrate, a betrothal, a wedding, the naming of
a baby, or the coming-of-age party of a youth;
for it was the boy, not the girl, who had a
début in those days.

If none of these functions claimed a citizen
of the capital, he was likely to proceed to
one of the *fora* for litigation in the lawcourts
or for business connected with his own
finances, or to perform his official duties, if
he were a senator or a magistrate, or merely
to lounge about quite as Italians love to do
in the town piazza. We must remember,

moreover, that public buildings were always more public than they are today and were full of rambling throngs. So, too, were the miles of colonnaded ambulatories the convenience of which is more generally recognized by Italian architecture than it is by ours. Nor was the capital without its beautiful parks for promenading. If it chanced to be a holiday, our typical Roman would join the throng going to the theater, the circus or some public games, according as opportunity offered or fancy prompted.

Somewhere between eleven and twelve o'clock he was normally free to eat his luncheon. As a rule, this was a cold meal, but more substantial than the breakfast, including in addition to foods already mentioned, fruits, nuts, salads and meats. With some it must have been a mere snack such as people devour at lunch-counters and in the railroad restaurants. Whether the ancients went home for it, or often had to resort to the cookshops which abounded everywhere near the haunts of business and of pleasure, we cannot tell.

Travellers in Mediterranean countries are all familiar with the practice, especially observed during the hotter periods of the year, of devoting the middle of the day to rest, if not to sleep. Vexatious as it is to find an entire commercial establishment, bank or museum taking a siesta just when you wish to enter its doors, you come to realize that the custom is one of Italy's sane traditions. The urban populace really had to learn it from the rural, and business in court and senate does not seem to have stopped for it, as agricultural labor did. However, the fashionable came to accept it, and so we find in commodious homes even a differentiation of bedchambers into those for the siesta and those for sleep at night, and during the summer season Rome in some sections was almost as dead at noon as at midnight.[57] It was, indeed, a time when story-tellers had the ghosts of the dead appear, while our more careful contemporaries permit only wraiths of the living at such an illuminated hour.

If the morning was claimed for work, afternoon may certainly be said to have been devoted to play. Next, therefore, in the routine came exercise and the bath. Since baths, as a rule, were taken publicly in the company

[57] Alaric took advantage of this to capture the city in 410 A.D.

of friends, they were regarded as a social pleasure rather than as an annoyance imposed by the threat of ill health. After the bath men would indulge in a stroll, a loaf, a chat or any other mild amenity of human intercourse such as the southerner still lapses into so automatically that the supercritical are likely to call him a worthless idler many times before they awake to the fact that he is really living, instead of merely working himself to death in order to live.

By mid-afternoon,[58] the Roman of position was ready for his dinner, for which the exercise and bath had been an appetizing preparation. Its perhaps minimum length of three hours must not, however, be interpreted as a proof of gluttony nor even its prolongation to five or more; for, as we shall see, the succession of slowly-eaten courses was interspersed with much frolic, conversation and even professional entertainment. The fast set would follow this dinner with a drinking-bout in many ways resembling a German *Kneipe*, but, as a rule, the respectable citizen and all those whom age made cautious omitted this

[58] From *nona*, meaning the ninth hour, comes the Danish word *none* which means a " collation."

and retired at once to bed at what we should consider a rather early hour. The lack of our brilliant illumination saved Romans from much temptation to turn night into day, and, almost as important, the absence of instruments for measuring time with precision made our stop-watch and split-second type of civilization impossible.

IX. SOCIAL LIFE

BUT we must now take up in detail some of these various occupations of the day to which we have only summarily alluded. Fashionable life in the twentieth century compels attendance at many functions, some delectable, others depressing, afternoon teas, musicales, card parties, mixed dances, evening receptions and theater parties, which were unknown to the Vanity Fair of two millennia ago. Moreover, to gratify the gregariousness of man we have club-houses and other special buildings to which the great bathing establishments of Roman cities offer the only approximate parallel.

Let us consider for a moment the most important of our own amusements, dancing. This engages almost everybody nowadays who has two feet out of the cradle and at least one foot out of the grave. But Cicero, who moved in the best society of his age, could say of it: " Practically nobody dances when he is sober, unless mayhap he has lost his

mind." Our androgynous dances, even minus
" trot " and " hug " and " shimmy," would
have shocked Terpsichore to a mortal death
as being possible neither to masculine dignity
nor to feminine pudicity.[59] Even solo dancing that was probably much more decorous
than certain Oriental performances that are
by no means unknown to American respecta-
bility drew the censure of decent people at
the close of the Republican period as voluptu-
ous. In general, Roman parents anticipated
modern morality in deputing to the daughters
of others dancing that would demoralize their
own, and at home and on the stage enjoyed
without a qualm the talent and beauty of
hirelings. In having others do much of their
singing and dancing for them, except in so far
as they belonged to the ceremonies of religion,
they were unlike the Greeks who valued
highly personal accomplishments in both these

[59] Tarantism is just as endemic in the larger cities of
Italy as in our own, nor can the mania be attributed
today to any bites of the tarantula. As a matter of
fact, the famous Italian dance, the *tarantella,* probably
owes its name to Taranto, which anciently was a Greek
city. A woman who is *tarantata* may dance for three
whole days. It remained for asininity in our own country,
however, to conduct voluntarily Terpsichorean " Mar-
athons! "

[117]

arts. But these different attitudes towards social pleasures bring up the larger question of etiquette and gentle manners. Had the Romans already their inviolable conventions?

If Cicero or Caesar were suddenly to appear in a modern drawing-room, there might be embarrassment on both sides, but anybody familiar with the social life of their time knows that the old Romans would impress the assembled guests as gentlemen. Some of us suspect that they might at once become the dominant figures by reason of their personal magnetism and noble bearing, but their manners would, of course, be different. Even specialists in the Classics, however, unless they have directed particular attention to the matter, seldom realize what a code of etiquette already existed twenty centuries ago with exacting requirements. In fact our earliest Classical literature, Homeric epic, offers us in the meeting of Odysseus and Nausicaa a charming picture of fine manners. Long, long before our era, the socially insecure had to worry about what people would say of their behavior. Mrs. Grundy is a very old character — old enough perhaps to die. In the Roman metropolis the best bred of our race would

have offended occasionally, even as a lady or
gentleman will blunder among foreigners today, if untutored in their conventions. Table
etiquette would have tried us the most, but
there was also much ado about precedence.
But after all, these would be largely matters
of outward deportment and not dependent
upon qualities of the heart. The really significant fact is that the men — those, for instance, of Cicero's or Pliny's letters — were
dealing with one another with a notably
modern, I almost said Italian courtesy,[60] but
that might be saying too much. Of course,
they had their vocabularies of invective which
left nothing to be outdone by the proverbial
fishmongers of Billingsgate, but such vituper-
ation was a tradition in public oratory and no
more a criterion of the vilifiers' real nature
than much of the obscenity of ancient comedy
and satire is that of their authors. In general,
however, the Romans seem to have been denied the genial affections that came so readily

[60] One may safely appraise the quality of a tourist's
breeding by his estimates of Italian manners. For a dis-
cerning characterization we may refer to M. Carmichael,
In Tuscany, p. 11, and to G. B. Taylor, *Italy and the
Italians*, pp. 263–265. For the German point of view I
know no better reference than the interesting critique in
Victor Hehn, *Italien*, Chapter VIII.

to the Greeks and in this particular to be strange ancestors of the friendliest of modern peoples.

The one social entertainment to which in default of so many of ours they attached a major importance was the dinner-party. In fashionable society the evening meal was probably regularly a guest affair, even if there were no special occasion, such as a birthday, to celebrate. This is in sharp contrast with social life in present-day Italy, where dinner-parties are as rare an entertainment as they are usual in either England or America. The meal belonged, as we have seen, to the second half of the afternoon and to early night. If one would make it fashionable, he had to advance the hour set, so as to steal something from the business day. In the enjoyment of a dinner-party both sexes might unite, an impossibility in Athens of the fifth century B.C., where women were confined to a seraglio-like existence the last traces of which survive in modern Hellenic custom. For example, the afternoon refreshment in a semi-outdoor café which is such a regular and mutual pleasure to men and women in every Italian community, is reserved in Greece almost entirely for men.

Even more than the modern café the Roman dinner-party served as a newspaper, the only evening " daily " that society had; for the gazette posted by government authority was much too scanty to satisfy a race that has always been eager for the latest news. It was the interchange of opinions at table that most assisted the work of imperial spies when they were making Rome politically a hell to live in. Under some of the emperors, table conversation ran more safely to discussions as to which came first the hen or the egg, why Jews forebore the most delectable of food, roast pig, and which hand of Aphrodite Diomedes wounded.

The Romans adopted a Greek custom and allowed men to recline at meals, while requiring, until the more dissolute days of the Empire, that women should sit, except when members of both sexes were dining strictly *en famille*. They observed this difference also in banquetting their deities, laying the statues of gods lengthwise on the couch but setting the female figures upright. Children might sit on stools within the reach of discipline but where they would be the least bother to their elders.

The three couches of a dinner-set were

arranged around three sides of a square table, with the fourth open for convenience of serving. Three guests could recline comfortably on each, resting on their left elbows with that hand free to hold bread and using the other to feed themselves. It was proverbial that the number should not be more than the Muses nor fewer than the Graces, since more than nine persons would overtax the accommodations and fewer than three would result in unsociable isolation. If the number was inconveniently small for this *triclinium* arrangement, the host might use instead a semicircular sofa with a round table that fitted its curve, while a large party necessitated recourse to one of his bigger dining-rooms which held two or more triads of couches. Moreover, apartments with different exposures would be selected to suit the season of the year.

Monied aristocrats could further indulge their taste for display by employing tables of rare and beautiful woods, the value of which appears to have averaged much above anything in corresponding use today. A round slab from the citrus-tree sometimes cost over fifty thousand dollars. Sideboards were likely to be the only other furniture in the room.

These exhibited pottery and plate, the design and artistic decoration of which are still imitated.

Good usage permitted a gentleman to bring to a dinner-party one or more uninvited friends. Such a supernumerary was called his " shadow " but with no intent to express the effect that his arrival would have upon the spirits either of fellow guests or of the surprised host. In the ancient home, servants and reserves of food were alike too plentiful for him to cause either anxiety or a shortage.

Since places on the couches varied in honor, there was a chance for feelings both of pride and of envy. At a stylish banquet, a special servant, a sort of social secretary, we might call him, located the guests with all the delicate discrimination that modern snobbery could devise. The same functionary seems sometimes to have had the further task during the course of the meal of elucidating any culinary mysteries [61] that were set before the puzzled diners. While such an expert might

[61] Some protection might seem necessary against cooks who could manufacture anchovies out of turnips and mushrooms out of gourds. Since antiquity already had its advocates of vegetarianism, they might have been useful in restaurants for the herbivorous.

occasionally be welcome at a modern banquet, we should have missed at Rome, on the other hand, some niceties to which we are accustomed. Thus, there was no insistence on having individual plates, and probably no fork or knife with which to facilitate eating. These implements were reserved for the use of a carver, whose training in a special school with wooden models for practice might make him one of the most precious of slaves. He had to vary his gestures and professional flourishes to suit each viand that he carved, and his graceful attitudinizing actually won for him the same name that Latin uses for dancers. Incidentally this is one of the indications that the art of dancing was not concerned with the feet alone.

For his soup a diner might have the use of a spoon, if he did not prefer to sop it up with a hunk of bread, which then, as now in many an inn, might later feed the lurking dog. The only other use for the spoon was for an egg in the soft state, which otherwise defies neat consumption, unless one " drinks it," as the Italians say.

Nothing could be more absurdly unjust than to picture the dinner of normal Romans

of wealth and social standing as a scene of
wild license and beastly gluttony,[62] either because the guests might consume more than a
fifth of the day at the table or because Latin
satire has left us such lurid accounts of ex-
ceptional excess. When we read that even
such a pattern of propriety as Pliny the Elder
apportioned three hours to his dinner, although
he was so niggardly of his time as to continue
his literary studies actually in the bath, we
may believe that it was not gulosity but rather
sociability of some sort that was responsible
for the prolongation. As a matter of fact,
various diversions might be intermingled, such
as comic acting, dancing, music and recitations, all of which may accompany a modern
meal though with rather different purposes.
Thus, in the old days, as I have already
stated, the guests themselves would not dance,
so long as they retained the inhibitions of

[62] Voluntary vomiting of one meal to give room
and appetite for another was no more usual in society
than drunkenness is now, but our contemporary *cicerone*
loves to localize and picture that scene in some ruined
apartment that he is showing. I once saw humming-
birds in walnut shells in the refrigerator of a famous
American hotel, but they could not be justly termed a
common *pièce de resistance* at one of our banquets any
more than the heels of camels or the tongues of nightingales and peacocks were at a Roman imperial dinner.

sobriety, but they enjoyed performances by professionals. Nor could such men as Cicero, a master and a lover of conversation, have foreseen the utility of a hotel orchestra in rescuing diners from reciprocal stupidities at the small cost of drowning out a few sporadic utterances of sense. Much less could even such an ascetic as Cato have anticipated an age when the reading aloud of some spiritual book in a college refectory would be regarded as a desirable offset to the carnality inseparable from all eating. None of them could have guessed that the survivals of their customs would take such peculiar forms. No, Roman gentlemen did not have to save themselves from ennui or from overeating. It is true, of course, that in the quality of their conversational wit and wisdom they fell short of Greek symposiac standards and that " authors' readings " must often have equalled the tedium that after-dinner speeches now so commonly bring to all but the speakers, but it is equally true in spite of all the fulminations of sensational satirists that their table luxury was moderate when compared with much that escapes all censure from our present-day pulpiteers. Such matters are purely

relative, and the typical Italian, when judged
by our metropolitan standards of living, was
and he certainly still is a temperate, not to
say abstemious man.

The Roman began his dinner by an in-
vocation of the gods which may be likened
to the saying of grace, although the recognition of divine power on such occasions was
probably more universal in the pagan past
than in the Christian present. Guests who
had come to the party in their litters, as even
healthy men might with propriety by the time
of the early Empire, would already have their
house-sandals on, but persons who came on
foot had to take off their shoes at the door
and put on the sandals which their attendants
had been carrying for them. These were then
removed at the dinner-table, since good form
prescribed bare feet on the couches. During
the meal a man's own lackey cared for the
discarded sandals and to ask for them corresponded to calling for one's carriage today;
for putting them on was a sign of intending
departure.

After the removal of their sandals the
guests washed their hands in water brought
by the servants along with the necessary

towels, a finger-bowl system which was more justified where everybody was presently going to dip for his food into a common dish, as among some Oriental peoples of today. This washing was repeated after each course. Waiters brought in and removed the dishes by means of trays and cleaned the table at each replacement. The Romans did not come to the use of a tablecloth until napkins [63] had been long in vogue. The stealing of the latter by " kleptomaniacs " was such a common vexation as to be referred to in literature.

The floors of stone and cement were so easily washed that diners did not hesitate to throw on them any refuse from the table for the animals to eat or servants later to sweep up. A famous mosaic pavement has been preserved to us which pictures the remnants of a banquet so perfectly that one is almost tempted to pick up the bones, shellfish and lettuce leaves or scare away the mouse that is enjoying them. Under the Empire young aristocrats would use at ban-

[63] The guest's use of his napkin to carry away tidbits from a dinner-party aroused the satire of Martial, but I have chanced upon a rather close parallel in the experience that J. A. Symonds had in Venice, as he narrates it in his *Italian Byways,* p. 224.

quets a special dinner-dress of Greek origin called a *synthesis*. Dudes went so far as to put on a new one, of different color probably, for each course, a custom that luckily does not control the wearing of the Tuxedo even by a fool. During the Saturnalia, the festival of Saturn, which in many particulars resembled our Christmas season, men would wear their festive garment everywhere in place of the *toga,* along with the so-called cap of freedom.

The typical dinner was tripartite. First there was an appetizer, the like of which is still usual at a Swedish or a Russian banquet, although it was not so liable to sate instead of whet the desire for food as is that northern bane to the temperate eater. Next, at least three courses formed the heart of the meal, which was succeeded by a dessert which the Romans called the " second tables." Some of the appetizers of the first division might appear on one of our menus among the hors d'oeuvres, oysters, salt or pickled fish, raw onions and lettuce with various piquant sauces. But eggs also figured, which are rather filling, to say the least, and the drink was a mixture of wine

and honey, which also would seem to us anything but a whet. Wine was served during
the rest of the meal, too, but in a moderate
amount and regularly mixed with water; for
to drink it undiluted was reckoned a display
of barbarism. Italians (including some vend-
ors) still water it.

The dinner proper which now followed
consisted of meat and vegetables served in
three or more courses. The dessert of cake,
pastry, nuts and fruit was so sure to include
the last that a proverbial expression for the
idea " from beginning to end " was " from
the egg to the fruit," as we might say of a
modern dinner " from the oysters to the
nuts and raisins." The dessert was preceded
by a more formal tribute to the household
gods, an offering of the salted meal-cake and
a libation of wine.

The table of a Cicero or a Pliny would
certainly provide us with food at least as
palatable as we are forced to eat in the Classic lands if we stray from the beaten paths
of tourist travel. For frying they used to
use olive oil. The Italians still do, when
they can escape its imitations. In fact, olive

oil may be listed with bread and wine as the permanent staples of Italy's food supply. The extraction of the oil may be described in the same terms for any period of Italian history, nor can one see at a modern vintage much that is not pictured in ancient bas-reliefs. They still tread the grapes amid song and merriment and have not given up entirely the storing of the wine in goat skins or pig skins. One who has seen the latter process in Greece or Italy understands just what is meant by Matthew IX. 17: "Neither do men put new wine into old bottles: else the bottles break and the wine runneth out, and the bottles perish: but they put new wine into new bottles and both are preserved." The Roman, it is true, knew butter, but merely as a medicinal plaster. The same description would answer today for some that is served as food in capric regions, but neither milk drinking nor butter eating is usual with Italians. Cheese was common, though often made from the milk of animals whom we allow to retain it for their nursing young. Ewes, mares and buffaloes even now serve the Italian dairy. For sweetening purposes the ancients depended on honey, although sugar also was already known but as part of the pharmacopeia rather than of the cuisine.

We should furthermore miss various fruits and vegetables that are ordinary enough with us, especially tomatoes and potatoes. On the other hand, most of us forego certain viands still eaten with appetite in Europe such as dormice and young kid. Those who have eaten *capretto arrosto* know why Horace's tears for the kid he sacrificed were of the crocodilian variety. The Roman bill of fare might also include the flesh of cranes and of the wild ass. Snails [64] of both the marine and the land variety, sea urchins and mussels, and the ink or cuttle fish have never lost their popularity at least among such Italians as have little choice. The evidence for the use of macaroni is not convincing, although some believe that instruments for making this now national dish of Italy are to be identified among the finds of Pompeii. By the period with which we are chiefly dealing, home-made bread was

[64] They are esteemed the special delicacy for the celebration of St. John's Day.

uncommon. They depended for their supply upon the public baker, as is so universally the case today in Italy.

Speaking summarily we may say that the Italian used to be and still is, so far as he has been uncontaminated by luxury and foreign custom, a small meat eater.[65] The World War has given thousands of soldiers their first carnivorous cravings. Ancient armies indeed regarded the substitution of meat for grain as one of the hardships of a campaign.[66] A sort of porridge made of spelt was long as much the stock dish as macaroni is today, and it continued to be so among the poor, ages after most people had much enriched their diet. The vegetables make a lengthy list with beans, onions and garlic placed high. To be sure, the latter two lost caste, with an increase in refinement, and inspired abuse in literature that we wish might

[65] The problem of refrigerating food is still unsolved for much of southern Italy. Snow brought down from the mountains is often used for cooling purposes, even as it was in ancient days.

[66] We may note in this connection the experience of the Marchese Guerrieri-Gonzaga, a landlord of Mantova, who, so L. Villari, *Italian Life in Town and Country*, pp. 54–55, states, began to distribute meat among his peasantry, but he soon discovered that they sold it to buy *polenta* instead.

induce the modern peasant to a more temperate indulgence in them.

Some fruits that are now common in Italy
are due to importation and naturalization in
Roman times, such as pomegranate, almond,
peach, apricot and fig, but there was an
abundance of native growths also. The absence of oranges and lemons would have
attracted our attention most.

All kinds of fowl and feathered game
were popular, especially the peacock. But
the pig is the one animal that came to be
consumed more largely than any other, and
they spared almost nothing from the end
of his snout to the tip of his tail, esteeming
as especial delicacies parts that the fastidious
now ignore. Fish figured as food for the
rich, who used to raise their own in artificial
ponds at great expense as edible pets.

In the case of the *jeunesse dorée* and of
others who were loth to lose all the gilding
of youth a wine supper might supplement
the regular dinner, a poor imitation of the
Greek symposium. Although the Germans
had already achieved the concocting of beer
two thousand years ago, it had not yet
crossed the Alps, nor were the more alco-

holic beverages known at all. At their
drinking-bout the Romans sought to delay
the too speedy oncoming of a disabling in-
toxication by using a profusion of sweet
smelling flowers, there being a quaint fancy
that roses shared with an amethyst ring an
especial potency for this purpose. Besides
flowers scattered over the table and floor,
others would be worn in wreaths or garlands
around the head and neck. In a close room
the odor of these [67] mixed with the heavy
scent of perfumery and with the fumes of
the wine and lamps would prove too much
for a modern visitor.

There was an etiquette observed in drinking which reminds us of later inventions of
the bibulous. A cast of the dice determined
who should be master of the revels so long
as mastery was possible. This man of luck
probably prescribed the proportions in which
the wine and water should be mixed, the

[67] The modern Italian, while apparently less sensitive
than we to outdoor smells, is yet strongly averse to
the presence of cut flowers in the house, and prefers an
artificial bouquet, if he must have a floral decoration.
At the time of childbirth in particular women are
guarded scrupulously against the odor of either perfumery
or flowers, according to W. W. Story's *Roba di Roma,*
II. p. 501.

rules that should govern the drinking and the
penalties that must be paid by transgressors
and blunderheads. Everybody had to drink.
Toasts were pledged according to a ruling
that required a small ladleful of wine to be
consumed all round for each letter in a sweet-
heart's name. Neither amethysts nor roses
were of much avail where tributes to Cyn-
thia or Amaryllis preponderated over toasts
to Ida and Anna. Each glass had to be
drained at a draught. The presence of loose
women was by no means unusual, and the
Spanish and Syrian dancing girls would seem
to anticipate cabaret entertainments of recent date. Gambling was common and the
stakes ran high. The return of inebriates
through the dark and scantily policed streets
of Rome was a menace to belated wayfarers,
with whom they played the " Mohawk " and
" Apache," and no doubt increased the in-
somnia of the sleepless in their beds.

Second only to a dinner-party as a social
event must have been the bath and exercise
that preceded it. Presumably among the
majority of this world's inhabitants a bath
is regarded and often reluctantly regarded
as an unavoidable necessity. Even among

those who seek a weekly cleanliness the night before the morning into which they concentrate all their godliness, the periodicity is sometimes broken. Originally, among the Romans the dictates of health and the constraint of society rather than pleasure kept a man to his duty. The national costume left arms and legs exposed to the dust and dirt; its woolen material puts special compulsion upon the wearer in a hot climate to wash his body. Accordingly, the earlier Romans gave their limbs a daily bath, their body a weekly, or, to speak more accurately, in the country, at least, a bath for every market day. But towards the close of the Republic all this changed. Daily ablutions came to be recognized as an invigorating pleasure [68] which belonged to the routine of the day as much as the dinner itself which it regularly preceded. What is more, even persons who could afford to have comfortable bath apartments in their own homes would prefer the sociability of the public estab-

[68] Accordingly, it was no reflection upon a guest to greet him with the question " Won't you take a bath? " and men in power used to curry favor with the proletariat by giving them the use of baths and barbers free for a certain period.

lishments; for Italians seem always to have been a most gregarious people. Several of the thermal plants could accommodate a thousand and more at a time and satisfy their desire for any known kind of bath, plain, plunge, or shower. Of course, the therapeutic value of baths, especially of mineral waters and of hot springs, was recognized fully in antiquity. It was a fashionable " cold water cure " [69] that restored Augustus to health and killed his adopted son Marcellus. Moreover, by their time, massage was already available for those who were too fat or too indolent to better their circulation by activities of their own.

For the exercise which was the proper preliminary to the bath, Romans adopted all the inventions of the Greeks, quite as nations that are now backward in sports look to England and America for their equipment and instruction. Connected with the *thermae* they had ball-courts, wrestling-places and

[69] Although personal cleanliness is just as much the rule among the educated of Italy as it is among those of our own land, the Anglo-Saxon propensity to take a cold water bath every morning is an idiosyncrasy which, like walking in the sun, or, in fact any long walking for mere pleasure, an Italian finds it hard to understand.

stadia. For the social pleasures they provided gardens, lecture rooms and conversation
halls. Even libraries might form part of
the immense edifices. Such a resort calls to
mind certain casinos in European watering-
places. The person familiar with Rome
thinks at once of the stupendous remains
of the Baths of Caracalla or of Diocletian,
but similar plants of goodly size were to be
found wherever the influence of Rome pene-
trated.

Only a nominal bath fee was charged, less
than a cent for men, perhaps twice as much
for women, while children up to a certain
age received the encouragement of a free
admission. No bathing suits were worn. At
first the sexes had different baths or used
the same apartments at different hours.
Eventually, however, mixed bathing was
allowed; but for women this promiscuity was
possible only to such as no longer had any
decency to lay aside with their garments.

While any order of procedure prescribed by
individual inclination or by a doctor's advice
was permissible, a bather commonly passed
into a warm anteroom from the locker apartment where his own slave was expected in spite

of all diversions of gossip to guard, against the ever-present bath-thieves, the garments his master had taken off. In this warm *tepidarium*, as it was called, he started perspiration in preparation for the next chamber which made him sweat profusely, before he took in it his hot bath. He would avoid enervation from this by a cold bath in the next room, or, if he preferred some warmth of the sun, he would plunge into an open air swimming pool. A complete establishment would include an anointing room in which the bather finally was scraped with a strigil, rubbed down with towels, and then, to prevent catching cold, anointed with perfumed olive oil. In the disrobing room, when he was not unlucky, he again found his clothes. An extra, domed chamber with a heat exit at the top was also sometimes provided in which the bather could take a Turkish bath hot enough to sweat out original sin with a lifetime of accretions. These sudatories were, in fact, especially valued by invalids who wished to start their animalistic life over again in spite of their deteriorated machinery for self-indulgence.

X. AMUSEMENTS

HAVING spoken of the three regular pleasures of the day's routine, we shall next consider the various amusements which might engage much of the rest of a Roman's leisure.

However austere and grave we may imagine the Romans to have been during their early history when *gravitas* or moral earnestness would be high in the listing of the virtues and men interrupted the strenuous toil of pastoral and agricultural pursuits merely to initiate every March a military campaign of imperialism from which they returned only in time to gather in the harvest, the day came, long before the commencement of our era, when a love of amusement became a prominent characteristic of the people. It still is. One of the first and last impressions of the foreign visitor is the pleasure-loving nature of the Italians and furthermore their readiness to be pleased with very simple things. In truth, they derive from mere living a kind of childlike enjoyment and gaiety that are denied the Anglo-Saxon temperament. Americans, indeed, often remark with a touch of envy that the Italians never seem to have grown up. With this prolongation of youthfulness we may connect more virtues than faults. It is a quality that may be expected in a land where it seems to be Spring somewhere always. In a smiling country smiles ought to be infectious. Even the widespread mourning and excessive poverty consequent upon the World War have not entirely destroyed the Italian propensity to laughter and song. This is especially true towards the south where the struggle is less severe and the paucity of money probably a little more uniformly distributed. Only he who has listened entranced to the wild abandon of Neapolitan singing at midnight or in country districts to the *stornello* in its minor key as it passes from field to field, can quite appreciate this side of Italian character. Even where conditions are truly grievous, the normal Italian refuses to take them so. " *Pazienza* " is his favorite word of self-exhortation [70] and the facility with which he

[70] *Il mondo è di chi ha pazienza,* runs the Italian proverb.

smiles and slips into merriment accounts
for much of his unmatched racial charm.
There is plenty of wit and humor in ancient
Latin literature and its satiric turn has de-
scended to the modern people.

It is true, however, that the Italian has
always been less creative in his play than
some more staid races. He is prone to seek
his amusement from entertainment offered
by others. Even many of the games of
childhood that we have already mentioned
were of Hellenic derivation. In any case,
by the beginning of our era Rome had certainly become a wonderful amusement center.
Even the street corners and open squares had
their itinerant performers of every sort.
Singer, clown, prestidigitator, juggler, diviner,
story-teller, snake-charmer, gathered their
circles as readily as in Italian communities
today. What would bore to melancholy an
American crowd illumines Italian faces with
delight. Puppet-shows have a tradition of
two thousand years and more. But these
one does not need to be an Italian nor very
young to find highly interesting in their per-
fected form. Even opera is not beyond the
attainments of the *burattini*.

The importance of one goddess, Fortuna, among the deities of Rome may be gauged from the power and persistency of the gaming passion which she has fostered. Markings on pavements brought to light in various parts of Italy bear witness to the pastimes of ancient boys and loafers, and these can still serve for apparently precisely the same games of today. In truth, gambling enjoys unparalleled popularity among our contemporary Italians and provides through lotteries a chief source of revenue for the government. In many a home one is more likely to find a book of instructions [71] about the numbers that will win (composed, of course, by some philanthropist who forbears to enter the field himself) than he is to chance upon a Bible. The Romans of old gave an extra zest to gaming by prohibiting it by law. An exception was made at the time of the Saturnalia,[72] even as the straitlaced Puritans of England allowed indulgence in the corre-

[71] The ancients had their dreambooks, but the *smorfia* that tells you what numbers to pick for the *lotto* is rather an advance over anything that they possessed.

[72] This is not the place to note in detail the parallels between the celebration of the pagan festival and the customs of Christmas and of the Festival of Befana on the Eve of Twelfth Night.

sponding Chirstmas season, and as, at all times in the year, the elderly were granted dispensation of a little final wickedness before they died. All others in the community, however, while recognizing with the law the social perniciousness of the vice, enjoyed it themselves as often as they could escape the official eye. Betting was essential to the popularity of the chariot races in the circus, as it is to our sports of diamond and gridiron, and cock fights were held for something more than the excitement of seeing the feathers fly.

Dice were, of course, the most convenient implements for a " quiet game." Dicers used cubes with the same arrangement of pips as ours, but also astragals which had only four sides on which to fall. Loaded dice have been found, proving that players of old put more trust in a bit of lead judiciously placed than in prayers and promises to Fortuna.

The gambling game that can be heard from the greatest distance today is *morra*.[73] 'The two participants, usually in a ring of fasci-

[73] M. Graham, *Three Months passed in the Mountains East of Rome during the year 1819*, p. 153, compares it to a game played by children in England " Buck, buck, how many horns do I hold up? "

nated on-lookers, yell in unison the number which they respectively conjecture to be the total of fingers extended by both simultaneously from a closed hand. The din and excitement are startling to a foreigner who nears a group for the first time, and he soon comprehends why the law has at times banned *morra* as being too fruitful of violence and murder to be tolerated. The Egyptians were playing the game ages before the Romans. To judge by representations in Classic art, gamblers sometimes guarded against the perils of angry impulse by clasping with the unengaged hand opposite ends of a stick. This insured at least a moment for reflection before the fisticuffs began; it may, however, have been used merely as a tally-rod. A Roman proverb aptly declared that an honest man was one with whom you could play at flashing fingers (*micare digitis*) even in the dark.

Americans touring Italy are so often balked in their business or in their sightseeing by unexpectedly finding a building closed because of a secular or a religious holiday that they can readily believe that under the Roman Empire also holidays were two or three times as numerous as they are in the United States. By the middle of the fourth century, the calendar actually assigned one hundred and seventy-five days to public games. Religious festivals came, indeed, with such frequency that we may be sure that they did not always put an end to secular labor. Their effect upon business was probably more like that of the sabbath upon a present-day Italian community than upon a Vermont town. A *festa* provides a combination of trade, religion, eating and sport that the ancient would have found entirely natural.

Holiday seasons gave opportunity for the free public games that are so characteristic of the civilization of ancient Rome. It is hard for us to comprehend how the circensian, theatrical and amphitheatrical shows could ever have originated in attempts to gratify some deity at a festival; for from a Christian point of view their popularity appears to be almost directly proportioned to their degree of wickedness. And yet it was not until the fifth century and probably much later that gladiatorial shows were finally stopped, nor ought we to forget that even in this year of grace Terpsichore, Fortuna and other pagan deities would not be so very ill at ease at certain Protestant church entertainments.

In ancient Rome, however, the shows were not merely a public amusement, but an occasion for distributions by the emperor of valuable gifts and money, which reminds us of souvenir performances in our own playhouses. What is more, they constituted great mass-meetings at which the people could register their feelings upon public questions as emphatically as by any modern system of voting. The emperor, therefore, attended the shows partly to feel the public pulse.

Although the Italian has ever displayed an innate gift for improvization and dramatic expression, which is observable today in pulpit, court [74] and legislative hall hardly less than on the stage, the theater anciently enjoyed none of the popularity that it possessed in Hellenic lands, or now has, as the chief Italian pastime. The Romans always got more pleasure through their eyes. In the drama, comedy rather than tragedy interested the

[74] Ciceronian efforts to sway the emotions rather than the reason have not lost their power with judge and jury, and Pliny's delight in applause would have been amply gratified, could he have pleaded in some Italian courts. See Deecke, *Italy*, pp. 267 and 322.

mob, and by the inception of the Empire this
had to take the form of mime, pantomime [75]
or farce, if it were to gratify the public taste
for what was exciting and salacious. No other
nation of antiquity would have welcomed so
warmly our moving picture shows, especially
such pictures as the censors suppress.

Although the capital counted a city popu-
lation of probably a million at the time of
Christ, it possessed but three permanent
theaters, and, as a rule, plays would be given
only on festival days. These, curiously
enough, came more frequently in the heat of
summer than in what we call the theatrical
season. The three playhouses were all open
to the sky [76] except in so far as awnings were
occasionally spread as a special inducement
to attend. Moreover, they could be used conveniently for only daylight shows. Since
morning came to be the usual time for a per-

[75] As everybody knows, Italians possess an auxiliary
language of gesture that especially among the vivacious
southerners is a marvel of efficiency. The deaf and
dumb are much less seriously afflicted than they are with
us, being by right of birth adepts in silent speech. Stage
pantomimes are still highly popular in Italy.

[76] At Nîmes, Orange and Paris the ancient outdoor
auditoria have all been put to theatrical use successfully.
From one playhouse in Florence they simply remove
the roof in the heat of summer.

formance, matinée would not have been in those days a misnomer.

In the regular drama men had to play the rôles of women, as boys did in Shakespeare's day, but we know of no instance where a male had to play the part of a female temporarily disguised as a man, as in the case of Rosalind and Portia. The ultimate employment of face-masks made this androgynism easier and facilitated the assumption of several characters by one and the same actor. Before the introduction of masks, wigs of different colors also helped to identify, even at the great distances of playhouses that seated as high as ten thousand auditors, the red-haired slave, the black-haired youth and the white-haired father.

The stage setting was as primitive as in England in Elizabethan times. At the beginning of a play the curtain dropped into a slit at the front of the long, high and somewhat shallow stage, instead of rising. Thus the heads of the actors were revealed before their feet, a proper courtesy, even though the latter might be, as ever and anon today, the more intelligent and entertaining portion of their anatomy. The regular scene for comedy was

a street. Fronting on it were represented two
or three houses before which all action had
to take place. This would always be truer
to real life in Italy than with us,[77] for there
is scarcely any physical act or domestic employment that one may not sooner or later
witness with a house façade as the background.

Actors at Rome were slaves or ex-slaves
and accordingly the former used to be liable
to a flogging, should their histrionic efforts
fail to please, an encouragement to the betterment of the drama that has not altogether lost
desirability. The modern Thespian who only
within recent years has won the social recognition due his art may read with interest a
Roman municipal law which barred from certain positions of honor thieves, butchers and
actors, a tell-tale coördination.

Naturally players could command but small
respect from an audience that would include
nursing babies as well as noisy and inatten-
tive patrons of a larger growth, ready to leave
at a second's notice, if news came of some
more sensational counter-attraction outside.
Still, later, the great Molière had to contend

[77] No one could bring out the contrast with more
sympathetic charm than Mary A. Hopkins in her " Whom
the Land Loves," in *The Atlantic Monthly*, 622 (1922).

with similar difficulties, and Italian theaters even now admit nursing infants and persons potentially obstreperous. One of the worst evils was a claque such as French theaters still harbor, although fortunately partisanship now is rarely more than a comical combat of hissing and clapping and it no longer occasions the tumults and bloodshed that sometimes occurred in an ancient showhouse. Actors bantered their audience from the stage as in cheap plays today. In Ovid we find another rather modern note when he tells how the prettily dressed ladies of his time used to go to the theater to see the shows but no less to be a show themselves.

The seating in the playhouse involved discriminations which the privileged guarded jealously. In those days no keeper of a dive could sit next to a senator through the mere possession of money. But alas! women were assigned to the top of the auditorium, while boys were curbed by being seated next to their pedagogues. Soldiers and married plebeians also had their separate places. So too, bankrupt knights, we are told, a merry company! To make everybody more comfortable in the heat they sometimes sprayed the great overhead awnings with a pleasant-smelling saffron-water.

Akin to the dramatic exhibitions were certain public competitions in oratory, poetry and music which the Romans adopted from the Greeks along with athletic contests of a Hellenistic type. We wonder whether the singing-matches in improvised verse that have their vogue among certain classes of Italians are an unbroken tradition from antiquity. Their existence in the sixteenth century in the form of the *tenzon* is well known to scholars. Even bands of music play in competition now, and no community is too small to boast possession of one. Among the physical contests boxing alone could be made sufficiently thrilling to interest the Roman and that only by making the hand-covering a death-dealer through the insertion of metal knobs and even spikes in the leather thongs that composed it. As for the literary and esthetic entertainments, they always seem an acquired taste for the Nation of Mars, quite out of harmony with the Roman racial instincts.

The masses really felt more at home in the circus where in fact all classes congregated with unalloyed delight and men and women might chatter and flirt with a freedom that was handicapped elsewhere. In Italy horse-racing is of great antiquity [78] and the Palio at Siena twice a year demonstrates that it can still command the hectic interest of an Italian crowd, and if the winning horse shares in the outdoor banquet of the *contrada,* there is excellent Classical precedent for such hospitality. Ultimately ancient Rome devoted to the sport her most magnificent building, the Circus Maximus, in which from one to two hundred thousand spectators of both sexes assembled under the open sky.

The long running-space was divided for about two thirds its length by a wall, ornamented with shrines, statues, a central obelisk, etc. A short distance off from each end of this medial " spine," as it was termed, were the rounding-posts, three pillars rising from a base. Just as nowadays a far-seen bulletin-board keeps the careless spectator in touch with the progress of a football game, so in the circus they had seven figures of dolphins

[78] Only recently, I learn, Mussolini has revived the old Roman chariot-race as one of his means of making his countrymen more proudly conscious of their glorious past.

pivoted on a stand, the turning of which one by one indicated the number of circuits the chariots had completed of the seven required.

At the signal of the presiding officer four chariots, as a rule, but in some periods as many as eight or even twelve, were sent away from a series of small chambers or stalls at one end. The charioteers exercised their skill in blocking or fouling rival cars or in crowding them against the rounding-posts, since the smashing of a competitor's chariot was an incident likely to afford the most pleasurable of all thrills. Persons who would now lose all interest in a trapeze-performer or in a tight-rope dancer, should these bring their apparatus too near a soft mattress on the ground, can readily appreciate the attitude of the ancients. The driver maintained his foothold in the bounding car and controlled his horses, two, more commonly four, but sometimes six or seven or even more, with the help of reins that were fastened around his waist. Accordingly, if spilled, his only hope for life depended upon his cutting the reins as he was dragged along by the panicky horses, scrambling to his feet and dodging the following teams. For this emergency he carried a sharp

[155]

knife, stuck in the thongs with which his body and thighs were protected. A leather cap, shoulder-pads and shin-guards likened him to our players of the gridiron.

The element of partisanship which is such a factor in the enthusiasm of our schools and colleges at outdoor sports was provided at Rome by the racing syndicates which furnished the horses and drivers under contract with the giver of the games. The charioteers wore the colors of their corporation,[79] and the betting on the red or blue or white or green (and for a while gold or purple) would remind us of the evil side of our own intercollegiate contests, while the madness of the spectators over the victory found vent in an adulation of steed and charioteer that even a football hero might envy. Riot and bloodshed more than once figure in the history of ancient horse-racing with a record of thousands of lives lost. Bribery of drivers, a resort to sorcery, the poisoning of horses and during the race every conceivable trick were inevitable abuses where unscrupulous gamesters

[79] Mrs. H. L. Thrale describes in her usual lively fashion an imitation of this custom; cf. Mrs. Piozzi, *Glimpses of Italian Society in the Eighteenth Century*, pp. 159–160.

faced the alternatives of financial ruin or fabulous enrichment, and where successful jockeying brought the charioteer himself the sort of fame that a prize-fighter enjoys today and relatively quite as much money. It is a far cry from the Circus Maximus to the English Derby!

Besides the actual races themselves, there would be much to remind us of the modern circus. In the first place there was the spectacular parade of those who were going to participate. With the presiding magistrate, clad in the gorgeous garb of a triumphing general, at the head and with plenty of music to draw a crowd, it passed through important thoroughfares and around the race-course just before the contest began. In the procession were troops of horsemen, the chariots and charioteers, and, escorted by priests, the statues of the gods borne in special cars of state or on barrows, precisely as in Italian religious processions the image of the saint or of the Virgin rides on its *vara*.

While the spectators knew the joys neither of peanuts [80] nor of pink lemonade, they

[80.] The cry of the Sicilian selling these American delights " *Murricani!* " " *Murricani!* " would mean nothing

sometimes received a distribution of food from the emperor which would convert the crowd into one that looked sufficiently like the patrons of the sawdust ring. Moreover, there were some very modern performances of trick-riders, who leaped from one horse to another and performed other acrobatic feats as they galloped at breakneck speed, and of tame animals who did amazing things. We can understand how elephants, camels and lions might be put to harness — Had not Bacchus, Cybele and the rest taught them how? — but just how the first named beast was made to write Greek, we can only guess; for it is certainly more than we can any longer expect college freshmen to do.

The circus was also occasionally the scene of wild beast fights, the fascination of which can never be equalled by our animal trainers nor by anything seen in a modern menagerie. They were called the " morning show," because they were regularly staged in that period before the gladiatorial combats. While originally they may have taken the form of a

to Cicero, come to life once more, but he would surely recognize his name and the chick peas that gave it in the cry of the vendor of *ciceri*, sold piping hot from the portable stove.

hunt by experts or of contests between wild
animals turned loose in the arena, eventually
they became a nauseating butchery of often
defenceless human beings. A modern bull-
fight can give only a slight conception even
of what the dumb animals suffered. The
fighters might be criminals condemned " to
the lions " for heinous offenses against society,
but too often they were political or religious
offenders, and, as we know from our accounts
of the persecutions of the Christians, they
might include women and children. Much
ingenuity was expended upon making them
reproduce scenes from mythological or tragic
story which would involve their death by
some savage beast. Sometimes the emperor
with grim humor would institute among the
half-starved *lazzaroni* of his day a scramble
for all sorts of animals turned loose in an
artificial grove, anticipating by some centuries
the Neapolitan *cocagna*. These various shows
acquainted the populace with all the major
animals of our zoos, bears, lions, tigers, elephants, crocodiles and hippopotami. Readers
who have perhaps seen at most in all their
lives a score of lions can with difficulty imagine the din and terror when four hundred

of those kingly beasts were exhibited at a
single show to make the welkin ring with their
roars; but no one can doubt that centuries
of wholesale slaughter in Roman arenas are
responsible for the dwindling and actual ex-
tinction of some species of wild animals
around the Mediterranean basin.

The nearest modern parallel to these ancient
spectacles has been afforded by the bull-fight,
the national sport of Spain.[81] This has also
engaged women and children and has caused
the death of many brave men. It brings the
successful an unmatched glory in the community that has been coveted by even members
of the nobility, as the fame of being a gladiatorial champion used to be in Rome in spite
of the normal social degradation of the con-
testants. Moreover, the passionate concern of
the fair sex in the convalescence of a wounded
bull-fighter can only be likened to the feverish
interest of high-placed Roman women in the
heroes of the arenic contest. Even the match-
ing of beast with beast is paralleled now in the
bull-fights at Panama, where as a pleasing

[81] The dole-fed idlers of Rome demanded *panem et
circenses*, "bread and the circus races"; the Spanish cry
is *Pan y toros*.

variation a tiger is sometimes let loose upon the bulls. Nor must we forget that cockfights still have votaries in all parts of the world, although nowadays the police sometimes add an excitement that is neither anticipated nor welcome.

Animal hunts, however, as well as gladiatorial exhibitions more commonly took place in the amphitheater, a monument peculiar to Roman barbarism to which we now turn. The Colosseum at Rome is, of course, the best known among the many that existed in all parts of the empire. Situated in the very center of the capital, it stands as the most lasting and incriminating memorial of all her public amusements.

The elliptical arena was edged by a fifteen foot wall. This might be faced with revolving rollers to prevent the wild beasts of the show from mingling with those in the seats to the disadvantage of the latter. In some amphitheaters a ditch of water ten feet wide further protected the spectators from any possible leap. Running up to a top the height of which must be seen in order to realize its full impressiveness, were tiers upon tiers of seats, which accommodated some forty-five thousand people, and there was standing room in the edifice for several thousand more.

We must expect to discover in any ancient people a certain amount of barbarity and cruelty, nor is it difficult for us, looking critically at certain institutions of the Romans and forgetting charitably a few of our own age, to make unfair comparisons. Gladiators were in great part prisoners of war who received a chance for life instead of being executed outright, as occasionally they still are among nominally Christian soldiers, or of being sentenced to a mere existence of ignominious servitude, an alternative almost as bad as death. Of course, when foreign wars ceased to recruit the ranks of these professional fighters sufficiently, the Romans increased them by condemning the worst of their criminals to the gladiatorial schools, nor can we forget that not only non-combatants taken in war and, in time of persecution, peaceful Jews and Christians, but also victims of petty or baseless charges in the law courts were added in order to keep up the ever dwindling number.

The Romans adopted this institution from the Etruscans as a funeral ceremony under the persuasion that the souls of dead men liked blood, but under the Empire gladiatorial contests had become a public show which the people would owe to the generosity now of some private citizen, now of a magistrate and again of the emperor himself. In other words, the exhibitions were often as much a political device to curry favor with the proletariat as a free band-concert or the like can be today. The reader will further recall how at the close of the Republic companies of gladiators which politicians maintained terrorized the capital as bands of gunmen have sections of American cities.

The number of those who were entered in a single show might be many hundred. They had received careful training in special schools. Although the business men who ran these were gratifying a passion more general and compelling than even that for drink today, they were as far from being reckoned philanthropists as saloon keepers have been in recent ages, and they suffered from the ingratitude of beneficiaries a similar social ostracism. Eventually the business became extensive, so that the state had to assume some of it and provide public training-schools. The discipline, diet, exercise and special instruction of these institutions made them comparable to modern military academies with the intellectual side omitted. The finished product was an expert brute, who might, however, retain a sufficiency of human feelings and sentiment to make him loth to kill one of his own schoolmates in the public duel. But it was a case of kill or be killed; the Roman mob did not assemble to witness any hesitations of affection. Gladiators usually fought in pairs, but more rarely troops of them were used to represent better the encounters of actual warfare. To encourage partisan interest and produce variety, the combatants received different accoutrements, fighting as Samnites or Thracians, with the net or lasso, heavy-armed or with a sword in either hand, on foot or in British war-chariots, blindfolded or handicapped in some other way, according as the ingenuity of cruelty might contrive. Even dwarfs and women were introduced to quicken once more the reactions of the jaded spectators.

Modern art has acquainted the layman with the scene as the Classicist pictures it to himself. After the opening procession around the arena, during which gladiators might pause before the imperial box and utter the fateful words " About to die, Emperor, we salute you," came the series of combats. First were sham fights with which the populace had but brief patience, then the encounters to a finish with real weapons of death. Slackers were driven to the slaughter by the shrieks of indignant spectators and by the whips or hot bars wielded by attendants. And it was worth while to win popular favor by a spirited contest; for it gave the defeated a chance for life. As soon as the victor had his victim prostrate beneath his pointed sword or dagger, the latter raised his finger as a plea for mercy to the presiding officer of the games. This official generally referred the decision to the spectators who made clear by cries and signs whether the vanquished man was to receive the death-thrust or a release to fight some other day. In the former case he was at once dispatched and his corpse was dragged off the arena as ignominiously as a dead horse in the Spanish bull-ring. The gore-drenched spot where he died was sprinkled with sand, not to obliterate the reminder of a frightful horror but to prevent subsequent fighters from slipping.

A series of signal victories and rising

popular favor might win the gladiator his freedom. In token of this, he received a wooden
sword, such as he had originally used as a
tiro in his fencing lessons in order to avoid
the danger of wasting a man in a death out
of sight of the public view. Gifts and prizes
might make him a man of means, nor did he
lack a certain social acclaim from the masses
such as a prize fighter still may win in our
country.

In the arena of amphitheaters, as well as
in natural lakes and in artificial ponds exca-
vated for the purpose, the Romans also exhibited the spectacle of a naval engagement
which might require the participation of
thousands of marine gladiators apportioned
between two fleets to represent the forces of
such historic enemies as *e.g.* the Athenians
and Persians. The alternate flooding and
drying of the Colosseum within the same day
was regarded as little short of a miracle in
hydraulics. The realism of these bloody naval
battles was occasionally heightened by the
introduction of sea animals in the water.
There were other aquatic exhibitions in which
nymphs and sea deities were represented in

their favorite element enacting the rôles accorded them by mythological story.

From even this brief sketch of the public games of the Romans the reader may estimate the inordinate interest which they took in exciting entertainments. We know that the possibilities of the contests, the qualities of the champions, and the tragedies that were inevitable were common topics of conversation among high and low. The interruption of business in great legislative bodies of England and America to follow the course of an international prize-fight has therefore ancient precedent. The contents of homes in antiquity attested the owner's special interest in the games, the frescoes he gazed at on his walls, the smaller ornaments, the lamps he carried in his hand, by their portrayal of scenes in circus, theater and amphitheater. Moreover, Pompeian housewalls disclose advertisements that are the precursors of present-day billboard posters.

XI. TRAVEL

FINALLY, we may turn to some nobler and brighter aspects of pleasure seeking. The traveller in Classic lands who ventures into out-of-the-way districts, in default of even the humblest hostelry, will often receive from private persons a hospitality [82] which recalls vividly to him the importance of that virtue in antiquity. Anciently natives of different countries formed ties of hospitality with each other which were reckoned so sacrosanct that remissness in their observance was a sacrilege and exposed the guilty to punishment by the supreme god himself. The use of the same Latin term for both host and guest (a phenomenon perpetuated in French and Italian), indicates the reciprocal character of the relationship. The two were under

---

[82] Even an Italophile must admit, however, that in these days at least the Greeks attain the higher general level of hospitality, although the generous friendliness of the Italian to an American who is at all *simpatico* is notable.

mutual agreement to entertain and protect
each other. They performed, in fact, duties
that fraternal orders now undertake for members, even to the extent of nursing and
doctoring the stranger. For the most part,
however, the bond called for no more than
housing and feeding and mayhap for some
assistance in business or in legal difficulties.
At the end of a visit, guest and host exchanged
tokens of hospitality, which might mean
merely sharing the parts of some divisible
symbol. These would be kept as heirlooms
in the respective families. The presentation
of a token even by a distant descendant of
the original benefactor would secure the un-
grudging grant of a similar favor from a
descendant of the first beneficiary. In the
absence of an inn — and no person of refinement would go to one anyway, if he could
avoid it — a traveller felt free to ask for
shelter at the most commodious house in the
community, nor need he dread the rebuff that
would surely be his in our cities, where he
might have the help of a third foot to quicken
his descent of the front steps.

It would be a misconception, however, to
picture Romans swarming over even their own

country for the purposes of mere sightseeing. To be sure, they may be termed a travelled people but it was education, a physician's prescription,[83] official or private business that sent them abroad.[84]   Only occasionally before the second century of our era do we hear of trips for pleasure. In general, the Roman was as reluctant to leave " the hub of the universe " as a Parisian his beloved Paris. *Campanilismo* is no new sentiment in Italy. Rome was life. When business or climatic conditions did call him away, he maintained as close connection as he could with the capital by correspondence, sending special couriers of his own as well as employing every other means of getting a letter through.   In the absence of a public post-office system, travellers were always acting as letter-carriers.   If important, he would send a duplicate through different channels and the contents might be concealed

[83] Doctors are only following the directions of colleagues two thousand years dead in sending consumptives for the milk cure to Castellamare near Naples and other patients to various medicinal springs that have never lost their reputation.

[84] In general the Roman would sympathize with Dr. Johnson's attitude towards voyaging: "No man who has contrivance enough to put himself into jail will go to sea in a ship."

in cipher. Post-office, telegraph and telephone systems make it more possible for a business man to remain at home than anciently, when men had to meet each other for oral discussion, explanation and bargaining.

For sea-travel the wealthy few had their own private yachts, but almost everybody had to depend upon the sporadic sailings of coasters, vessels so small [85] as to be a guarantee of seasickness, and so likely to blow astray that, lacking the compass, they could attempt short cuts through the open sea only in the best of weather. The Greeks, not the Romans, were the sailors of Classical antiquity. On land, of course, the traveller fared better, since the Roman road system has been equalled only recently and their vehicles [86] were at least no worse than those that still rack one's bones in rural districts. The real difficulty was to secure wholesome food and potable water, a vexation that continues to be serious in large sections of Greece and in

[85] This does not mean that there were not also large craft, such as brought the monolithic obelisks from Egypt and such as the grain-ships from Alexandria.

[86] It may be worth noting that the taximeter had its ancient prototype in the hodometer invented by Hero of Alexandria.

lower Italy. Of course, along the main roads of the latter country there was a sufficiency of inns, such as they were, and under the Empire trade centers would even have tolerable hotels for transients.

Tavern-names like "The Cock," "The Elephant" and "The Wheel" have a very modern sound, but there were no modern conveniences to be found in them. Moreover, the innkeeper could be called a Boniface only in irony, since extortion and cheating were his means of livelihood. His beds were hard and had numerous permanent occupants that made sleep difficult. Moreover, one's fellow guests might be of the rough sort and noisy, even though the wine were too well watered [87] to make them drunk. The smoke and smell of the interior also sorely tried the finical. We are not surprised, therefore, that men like Cicero maintained their own houses of call and private villas in many parts of the peninsula. Thus an interchange of courtesies would always facilitate the travel of the well-to-do, while any errand on state business assured

[87] There was an astrological joke to the effect that taverners were born under Aquarius the Waterman.

them shelter everywhere either in the imperial
post-houses or through the hospitality of local
magistrates. But besides the robbers who
worked in the guise of innkeepers of both
sexes, there were also the professional bandits
and highwaymen to fear. From them even
arms and a retinue did not always save the
wayfarer. By way of compensation, however,
the Romans in most parts of the empire would
escape the rapacity of the money changer; for
his own coin was almost world-currency.

The traveller could divide a long journey
into stages, since outside of every town-gate
he counted on finding a public stable. Draft
animals ranged in size from the horse down
to the diminutive donkey and in disposition
from the mild ox to the mean mule.[88] Ancient
pictures show us a saddle similar to the struc-
ture of wood that the peasant now imagines

[88] Italian animals have to bear much the same bur-
dens and abuse that they did in the days when Horace
used to gall the haunches of his stumpy mule with his
baggage and its shoulders with his corpulent self. While
the Sicilian blesses the ox for having, with its fragrant
breath, warmed Christ in the manger, he never forgets
that the ass ate the straw out from under Him; nor lets
the *asino* forget it either. Cf. E. P. Heaton, *Bypaths of
Sicily*, p. 174.

adds to his comfort on a donkey. Naturally
the Roman was slow to resort to horseback,
if he could possibly procure one of the two-
or four-wheeled carriages that were then in
use. For shorter distances comfortable litters
and sedan chairs were also available.[89] As
one reclined in the former, he might pull its
curtains together and take a nap. These con-
veyances came to great popularity among the
rich of Rome where traffic laws forbade the
use of vehicles during most of the daylight
hours. Even a palanquin borne by four to
eight burly slaves, preceded by footmen to
clear the way and followed by a considerable
cortége of flunkies and dependants, could find
no easy passage through streets that averaged
not much over fifteen feet in width. But to
the highways and byways of an ancient town
we can give some special attention only
after we have paid a brief visit to a Roman
vacation home.

The excursion of the well-to-do to some

[89] To what extent persons susceptible to seasickness
suffered in them, we can only surmise. Even a pope
has had difficulty to stomach his in the inaugural procession; cf. Headley, *Letters from Italy*, p. 118. The use
of a *lettiga* suspended between mules has only recently
become obsolete in Sicily, if, indeed, it has. It recalls
the *basterna* that bore the fine ladies of imperial Rome.

family villa by the sea, in the country or among the mountains would have been much more formidable, had they not kept such places furnished and equipped with slaves ready for their instant reception. Men of fashion possessed them in widely separate parts of Italy so that they had only to consult their physical comfort at any season of the year. To own one was really the sole way to secure a holiday recreation, in the absence of the great resorts and " cures " that now cater to thousands of every class. And yet how much less necessary a vacation must have been for city-dwellers who (in Rome at any rate) had the purest of air and water and a life that was so much less complex and hectic than that of urban America! Of course, some resorts drew not merely because of their wholesomeness but because they were centers of fashion. For instance, Baiae in March and April was a sort of Newport in the season. Antium was a watering place of imperial fame, the birthplace of two emperors, Caligula and Nero, and it is still Rome's favored sea-resort.

The plan of a villa varied according to the degree that it was to be used as a mere pleasure home or at the other extreme as the farm house of a productive estate in the country.[90] We are told that the peristyle part of the building was put at the front instead of behind the *atrium*, as it was in city-dwellings. Windows were more numerous and larger and open *logge* were often a feature, as in the upper story of Italian palaces now.

A gentleman's villa cared not only for the physical side of man by its baths, exercise grounds and garden promenades but for his esthetic and intellectual interests by libraries and art collections. Great attention was paid to the beauty of the parks and gardens, and in villas by the sea there were shore constructions extending far out into the water. The tides in the Mediterranean are so slight that the scenery was not marred by the exposure of mud flats twice a day, as upon so much of our Atlantic coast. The sea is so salt that its clarity and blueness are almost unexampled elsewhere. Prospect towers, porticoes, embowered pavilions, fish-ponds, canals and aviaries were embellishments of the larger

[90] The resemblances between Roman and modern Italian farm life are too numerous to discuss here. The *fattoria* with its activities, from those of the bailiff down to those of the wide-horned oxen, afford our best commentary for the writings of Cato, Varro and Virgil.

estates. Landscape gardening was formal in
its treatment of shrubbery, trees, flower-beds,
trellises, grassy terraces and covered walks.
Italy's characteristic trees, the pine and cypress, are so architectonic that they may have
originally dictated the style. In any case sym-
metry and artificiality have remained the
Italian tradition.[91] Roman gardeners clipped
the box to form names and geometrical de-
signs. The latter were not only cones and
pyramids of vegetation but even imitations of
animals. Thus they showed a truly Japanese
delight in dominating nature and subduing it
to the hand of man. Vacationists amused
themselves by holding boat races or by merely
basking on the beach, as they still love to
do at Capri and on the Lido of Venice, by
pleasure rows and swims, and by hunting [92]

[91] In spite of this formalism villas are often of an
exquisite beauty. It is no outrage to realism if Botticelli
or Filippino Lippi people an Italian garden with angels
when nightingales send out the invitation.

[92] There is much use of decoys in Italy, since bird
life has been so largely shot off. Those who have seen
in Tuscany, a small owl fettered at the top of a long
pole which is raised high in the air that his puzzling
antics may attract other birds through their curiosity
and bring them within gunshot, may be interested to know
that the *civetta* is a long-suffering animal, having served
hunters similarly thousands of years ago. The birdlime

and fishing excursions. Literary men, however, cared most for these retreats as making possible intellectual discussions and the reading and writing of books. How difficult the latter must have been in the metropolis, we can better imagine after we have given some examination to the outdoor life of the populace.

and the nets that Italians use are an equally old invention in their land. The Roman never was a sportsman in the English sense of the term. The letters of Pliny the Younger alone offer a sufficiency of melancholy evidence of this.

XII. STREET–LIFE

A MAJORITY of town-dwellers two thousand years ago seem to have spent a minimum of time within doors. The climate has always enticed the people out of their houses to do as much of their work as possible under the open sky. This accounts perhaps for that indifference to domestic comforts that impresses pampered American visitors so profoundly. Naturally, Romans whose means permitted them the possession of a house with a courtyard could enjoy both fresh air and privacy, but the majority must have overflowed upon the public thoroughfare quite as they do in the humbler quarters of modern Italian cities. There you may see the cobbler mending shoes, the basket-maker weaving osiers, the butcher selling roast meat from an entire spitted carcass, the baker neatly laying out his loaves of dough on the road-bed, or, worse still, the manufacturer of macaroni hastening the drying and increasing the weight of his wares by exposure to the swirling dust. As for the other sex, who has not seen that most charming and gossipy of women's clubs, the gathering at the village fountain and washing-tanks? Furthermore, all the operations of spinning wool and carding flax are on public view, not to speak of such intimacies as the nursing of the baby,[93] the combing of their own beautiful tresses or the absorbing search in the thick hair of their children for undesirable inhabitants with just the patience that monkeys show in the zoo during a similar interchange of courtesies. These scenes must be of immemorial antiquity and there are many more that are like them. Thus, the schoolmaster of old taught and spanked his pupils in the open air. They still do at least the former in Italian rural districts. Nor can we omit from this list the beggar, ever ubiquitous in Italy. His methods have not changed in twenty centuries. Hill-slope and bridgehead are still his favorite sally-points.

Moreover, you may answer a business advertisement in the newspaper for number 12 on so-and-so street only to find that contiguous houses are 10 and 14 and that an enterprising

[93] Italians of humbler position will do this in either theater or art gallery; prudery about motherhood is not noticeable anywhere in Italy.

financier has taken 12 to represent his place on the sidewalk from which he greets you, as beyond a doubt his looked-for customer, as he sees you examining the houses in perplexity. So, of old, Martial tells us how Rome had become one big shop through the transfer of business from the interior of buildings, where at least some of it belonged, to the sidewalk and street, where it blocked all movement of pedestrians until the law interfered. Whole streets were anciently given over to special trades, just as now in Italian cities you will find a *Via dell'Argenteria,* a *Via dei Calderai* and the like. In the absence of our great mercantile establishments, much business was carried on by hucksters and peddlers, whose street-cries are still echoed closely enough by their descendants, especially in Italy's southern cities. Cake and cookie shops served the sweet tooth then as now, and names of wines that make music in the odes of Horace can still be heard in the *locanda* or *trattoria* that represent well enough the old *caupona* and *thermopolium.* Barber-shops and doctors' offices were the favorite lounge just as today in small towns barber-shops and the apothecary's.

[181]

Most of what has been said concerns primarily the ordinary people, the tunic-clad throng, but even the gentleman of two thousand years ago who did no manual labor haunted the public squares and porticoes, transacting business, interchanging gossip and learning the news. The circulation of canards under the early Empire was no small amusement. They called it "selling smoke." Indeed, the traveller, fresh or, let us·rather say, tired from the strenuous life of New York or Chicago, will never appreciate how busy a pleasure-loving, sociable people can be in doing nothing under a sunny sky, until he has himself seen and tried to live the café life of a Greek or an Italian city. It is the sight of this that usually leads to the sweeping condemnation of an industrious nation as loafers. City life offered the Romans the same temptation, and towards the end of the Republic the capital had gathered in thousands of a once universally sturdy and hard-working race who could now say in all sincerity *dolce far niente*.

But it would be a serious mistake to imagine that members of the upper classes lived indolently. Their social life alone was a busy leisure sufficiently exacting to put them in a fever of restlessness to which we often have reference in the literature of the time. There was much running from town to country and from villa to villa without finding the relief of peace and quiet. This is modern enough. On the other hand, the city-dweller of today would have noticed in ancient Rome the absence of night-life due to the slight illumination of the streets. Torch or lantern is still necessary in many a village of Italy, if one would dare the uneven and too often unsanitary streets after dark. But circulation through the narrow thoroughfares of ancient Rome required a retinue of armed slaves and torch bearers to make it safe also from footpads and riotous young blades. The latter were quite as belligerent as the highwayman but they expected their social standing to save them from any evil consequences, quite in the spirit of some of our college boys.

Of the capital by day we cannot have a vivid picture without visualizing the processions of all sorts that were frequently parading the streets. They made Rome as gay and picturesque as modern Italian cities periodically become for the same reason. We may even surmise that a passion for them is a birthright of this people. Those of old made a long list, triumphal, lustral, priestly, nuptial and funeral. Even the appearance of a praetor or a consul with his necessary lictors and attendants made a show. Sometimes details of the pageant of today strike the Classicist as an astonishing reproduction of the old; the tonsured priests of Isis come to life once more, torches or candles again flare in the street, reversed, it may be, as a symbol of mourning, a sacred image rides high on its *vara,* shouldered by those who are faithful to another belief but with no less pride in their function.

Of festal life in the thoroughfares we have but little information, but we hear of great outdoor banquets like those that follow the Palio at Siena and, to a less degree, like the street feasting of the Piedigrotta at Naples. Rustic celebrations, on the other hand, are more fully described, and such seem a forerunner of the revelry, color, song and merriment that we associate with the southlands of today. One thinks, for example, of the return of the pilgrims from Monte Vergine to Naples or of the somewhat Lupercalian, if not Bacchanalian, features of the Feast of Saint Alfio at Catania.

Roman streets were free from some perils that now infest them, such as our vehicles of harnessed lightning, but they provided a sufficiency to discourage any sleep-walking. Upstairs lodgers had a habit of throwing refuse from a window without calling out to the wayfarer or even confining the cast to objects decently dry. The tourist in Italy who has never been hit by a similar downpour has had luck. Moreover, in the old days houses used to fall down and conflagrations were a scourge. Juvenal classifies such fires and collapses with the interminable recitations of authors as typical city dangers; so they must have been pretty bad.

XIII. BURIAL

DURING the course of this little treatise my reader may have been able to create for himself a somewhat shadowy figure of an old Roman. It is now time to put what there is of him out of existence as quickly as we may and give him a decent funeral. One is tempted to say that if the ancients had not died, they would not have lived, so true is it that we owe an immense amount of information about them to what they depicted and deposited in their tombs. Obviously some sort of belief in immortality was general or else they would not have laid away so many objects of utility and ornament at no small financial sacrifice. A study of customs concerned with the death of a Roman is therefore unavoidable in any treatise on his life.

According to a conviction of that age, a ceremonial burial of the dead was requisite, if the soul was not to haunt the home of the living, unhappy and causing unhappiness.

They carried their persuasion of this so far
that where the corpse itself could not be re-
covered, they would still gratify the spirit with
its due funeral rites and perhaps erect a ceno-
taph for it. Furthermore, the man who found
the body of a stranger and failed to scatter
over it at least the three handfuls of dust that
constituted a ceremonial burial was sure to
suffer for his sinful neglect.[94]

In the Italian peninsula the shifting of custom between cremation and inhumation is an
important chronological and ethnological test.
If the Romans may be said to have begun
with burial, it is one of the many examples of
their notable conservatism that even during
the period that we are especially considering
when burning the remains was the prevalent
mode, a small portion of the body, commonly
a finger bone, would still be interred. Babies
who died before they were forty days of age,
slaves, the very poor who could afford neither

[94] One wonders whether he sees a survival of that
custom in slightly changed form when the nomadic
laborer of the Campagna bares his head before a cairn
that marks a nameless grave, throws at least one stone
upon the pile, and then, crossing himself, proceeds on
his lonely way. The practice is noted by A. Cervesato,
The Roman Campagna, Translation by L. Caico and M.
Dove, p. 80.

coffin nor funeral pyre, and those who had excommunicated themselves by conversion to Christianity were all disposed of at death by inhumation. Criminals had their carcasses exposed to the mercy of the heavens and of its most repulsive creatures, the carrion birds, in the " Potters' Field " of Rome. This was, in very truth, a loathsome place. There were great burial pits, not unlike those that were still in vogue in Italian cemeteries up to recent years, into which were dumped the refuse, the bodies of animals and the pauper dead of a city numbering a million souls. Hither resorted not merely carrion beasts and other scavengers, but the scarcely human witches to secure the implements of their magic. Ultimately, in the Augustan age, considerations of civic hygiene compelled the covering of it with a heavy layer of earth and its conversion into a sanitary pleasure park.

Roman law required cremation and burial to take place outside the city walls. This accounts for the long lines of tombs at the side of the roads radiating from the capital and from Pompeii, memorials of human pride, suffering and affection, but indicative also of a belief that the dead liked to lie near life and the living and that survivors perhaps were not so averse as the sensitive are now to being reminded constantly of death.

The external architecture of the Roman tomb would be no novelty in any of our burial-grounds, although it is rather such cemeteries as those of Genoa and Naples that best reproduce the forms of monuments that once adorned the famous Via Appia on either side for many miles. The flower-beds and trees that were often planted around them would also make them look familiar, but the interior was frequently decorated, furnished and illuminated much as a dwelling for the living. This is paralleled by some Italian sepulchral chapels with their pictures and busts and the ever-burning lamp in front of the figure of the Madonna. The sculpture outmatches even Roman realism. I am informed that at the dwellings of the dead in the Campo Santo of Milan the faithful leave their visiting-cards on All Souls' Day as evidence that they have called. Besides the private sepulchres of the Romans there were burial-places provided on a large scale by joint stock companies and by other corporate bodies. Some of these were like the funeral guilds of modern Italy. Already at the commencement of our era they were numerous and powerful. By regular contributions and coöperative management members assured themselves of a respectable funeral and of a final resting-place that would content their ghost. The *columbaria* which they constructed received this name from the resemblance of the rows of niches in which the cinerary urns were set to the nests of a dove-cote. In Italian sepulchral buildings, however, the places to receive the bodies are most like those in the Christian catacombs.

As a man lay dying, a near relative might kiss his lips to catch his soul as it issued with the final breath. When the end had come, those assembled would utter a wail, calling him by name,[95] a custom traditional probably from a time when such an address and such keening would be regarded as a real criterion of whether life was extinct or not. The eyes were then closed, the body washed, annointed and laid out on a funeral couch in the *atrium* to look as natural and impressive as possible in a *toga* and with whatever insignia of dis-

[95] Similarly after the death of the pope the Cardinal Camerlingo, tapping the dead man's forehead with a silver mallet, thrice calls him by name, and then receiving no reply declares him dead.

tinction belonged to him in life. The feet
were directed towards the door [96] to symbolize
his approaching departure on his last journey,
and a penny might be put between his teeth,
the fee for Charon's ferrying across the Styx.
This practice is still continued to some extent
in Greece and sporadically in Italy, although
the contents of graves for thousands of years
have disclosed a surprising neglect on Charon's
part to collect such fares. At the front door,
reminding us of the hanging of crape, were
branches of cypress or of pine which served
to warn callers that the pollution of death was
upon that household. The lying in state of
a distinguished citizen might last for days but
the humble had the privilege of a quick burial
with all desirable simplicity.

The obsequies of a prominent man were
such a soul-stirring pageant as to constitute a
public entertainment for all who were not
personally afflicted by his death, nor can we
doubt that in a season of scarcity of the regular shows there were those who would yearn for
a funeral with its accompanying games. The

[96] This accounts for a strong feeling that Italians
still have against placing the foot of the bed they sleep
on in that direction.

marchers carried torches, a relic of the time when all burials were made after dark, but also a point of resemblance to the wedding procession which the cynical may have noted. The danger that something else beside the corpse might be burned at a funeral in Rome necessitated extra services from the fire-department in the narrow thoroughfares of the city. In the case of a public ceremony a town crier summoned to the parade by a set formula of words. An undertaker assigned places in line on the basis of worldly rather than of spiritual values. The instrumental music was enough to wake the dead, being blared by horns and trumpets and shrilled by pipes. But even this in early times had the vocal addition of hired mourners [97] who sang dirges and pulled at their hair as they marched along. Occasionally there would be a mummer to imitate the dead, to the no small amusement of the crowd. Actors were selected to wear the portrait-masks [98] of ancestors who had held curule office, not excluding even such

[97] I am informed that this practice still survived in the nineteenth century in certain parts of Italy.

[98] Death-masks of wax are used in Sicily but for a different purpose. Consult G. Pitré, *Catalogo Illustrato della Mostra Etnografica Siciliana* (1892) p. 83, No. 231.

legendary personages as Aeneas and the Alban
kings. It would seem, indeed, as if the dead
really buried the dead and with a pomp comparable only to that of the triumphal parade
of some general. And yet persons familiar
with Italy cannot fail to recall in this connection spectacular funerals conducted by the
confraternità, shrouded completely in white or
black except for eyes and feet, lighted by
candles comparable almost to torches in size
and accompanied by a band playing truly
sad but resounding music.[99]

Anciently, the corpse, with face exposed, as
it still is sometimes in Italian funerals, was
carried on a lofty bier escorted by family,
freedmen, slaves and friends, all in the dark
clothes of mourning (although white was
eventually the privilege of women) and many
of them tearing their hair, beating their
breasts and lacerating their cheeks amid
lamentations that made funerals as proverbial
for their fearful din as they are with us for
solemn hush. When on occasion Sicilians halt
the funeral cortège for the delivery of a eulogy
of the dead, they are following ancient prece-

[99] It was such a procession in Spain that Don Quixote
and Sancho mistook for a troop of devils.

dent. At Rome this took place in the Forum and the speech by a son or other close relative could be relied upon to laud the departed and all his ancestors beyond the recognition of the well-informed. Scholars suspect that panegyrics of this sort are the ultimate source of much that long passed for history with as little justification as have the traditions that are traceable to political pamphleteers and to professional satirists.

At the cremation of a body there was further opportunity for a costly ostentation which sumptuary laws proved powerless to stop. For, along with precious perfumes and spices, tokens of affection and expensive gifts were cast upon the pyre. This was finally lit by some relative who kept his face averted as he applied the torch. Water or wine was poured to quench the embers, a last pathetic farewell cried to the dead and all the participants were purified of pollution by thrice sprinkling with water. Only the immediate family still lingered to collect the ashes, sacrifice a pig to consecrate the place of burial, and then partake of food. At the house there was an offering to the *Lares* as the final lustration.

Nine days [100] of intensive mourning followed, in the course of which the ashes were transferred from a cloth in which they had been drying to an urn for deposit in the tomb. A sacrifice to the *Manes* of the dead and a funeral feast, at which the garb of bereavement was not permissible, closed this period. But one was expected to be in mourning for a near relative ten months, the length of the old Roman year, for more distant relatives eight months and for children between the ages of three and ten a month for each year of their age. Nor even then was the memory of the dead allowed to die; for there was an annual public festival corresponding somewhat to All Souls' Day,[101] as well as anniversary memorials of the birth or death of the deceased, not to speak of a ceremony in March when violets were laid upon the last resting-place of the dead, and another in May when roses

[100] We may compare the novendial period of mourning for a pope.

[101] The consumption of beans and of confections, *fave,* imitating their shape, that characterizes this season of the year at Venice, recalls the use of black specimens of this vegetable for the laying of ghosts so amusingly described by Ovid in his *Fasti.* There can well be a survival in this.

were similarly bestowed. All these were occasions for offerings to be made to the gods in their temples and to the spirits of the dead at their tombs where lighted lamps and the feasting of the survivors have their obvious modern parallels. A notable oblivion has, however, fallen upon the pagan practice of pouring through pipes that led directly upon the cinerary urn the good wines that the deceased had enjoyed in life. In the Christian heaven at least there seems to be an enforced prohibition. In general, however, there was a feeling that spirits in the other world should be well treated in this. Nor is this without parallel in modern nations. How familiar to the student of the Classics is the superstition current among the ignorant of Sicily, that after the earthquake had destroyed Messina the souls of the prematurely dead were seeking to enter the living in order to live out their abbreviated term of years and in wrath at their unfair treatment were responsible for destructive storms?

In fact, the lifeless relics used to be far more an object of solicitude than they are now. They even had to be safeguarded against the spirits of evil by putting away with them amulets such as are the magic nails so often found in Roman tombs. Having been present myself at the opening of a virgin sepulchre which the mourners of two millennia ago certainly thought safe against any tomb robbers, I know just how an archaeologist ought to feel and how powerless any prophylactics against evil really are. With which solemn thought we may take leave of our dead Roman with the usual *ave atque vale.*

BIBLIOGRAPHY

BIBLIOGRAPHY

No treatise has been written, so far as the writer knows, to connect Roman private life with that of Italy today. The following bibliography is selected to meet the needs of educated laymen who wish to study the subject more thoroughly. Since the large handbooks mention most of the other essential works, the writer hopes to escape any display of that bibliographical erudition which so often depresses the expert without adequately impressing the ignoramus.

For his fuller account the scholar turns to such works as:

BLÜMNER, H., *Die römischen Privataltertümer*[3], in Iwan von Müller, *Handbuch der klassischen Altertumswissenschaft*, iv, ii, 2. Munich, 1911.

MARQUARDT, J., *Das Privatleben der Römer*, 2 vols., Second Edition by A. Mau, in J. Marquardt u. Th. Mommsen, *Handbuch der römischen Alterthümer*, vol. 7. Leipzig, 1886,

and to the special articles in:

BAUMEISTER, K. A., *Denkmäler des klassischen Altertums*. 3 vols. Munich, 1889.

DAREMBERG, C., et SAGLIO, E., *Dictionnaire des Antiquités Grecques et Romaines*. 5 vols. Paris, 1877–1919.

PAULY, A. F. VON, WISSOWA, G., KROLL, W., *Real-Encyclopädie der Classischen Altertumswissenschaft*. 13 vols. (incomplete). Stuttgart, 1894–1922.

DE RUGGIERO, E., *Dizionario Epigrafico di Antichità Romane*. Rome, 1895 seq.

Brief but useful, particularly for the bibliography under each heading, is:

LÜBKER, F. H. C., *Reallexikon des klassischen Altertums*[8], herausgegeben von K. H. J. Geffcken u. E. Ziebarth. Leipzig, 1914.

Valuable also are various chapters in:

BIBLIOGRAPHY

CAGNAT, R., et CHAPOT, V., *Manuel d'Archéologie Romaine.*
2 vols. Paris, 1916–1920,

and, for various special topics that have been slightly
treated in this book:

BLÜMNER, *Technologie und Terminologie der Gewerbe
und Künste bei den Griechen und Römern.* Leipzig,
1887. New edition of volume I, Leipzig, 1912.

GRASBERGER, L., *Erziehung und Unterricht im klassischen
Alterthum.* 3 vols. Würzburg, 1864–1881.

Those who read German readily will enjoy:

BAUMGARTEN, F., POLAND, F., WAGNER, R., *Die Hellenis-
tisch-Römische Kultur.* Leipzig, 1913.

PERNICE, E., *Griechisches und Römisches Privatleben,* in
A. Gercke und E. Norden, *Einleitung in die Altertumswissenschaft,* II. i. Leipzig, 1910.

On the other hand, the reader who has only English
at his command may resort not only to the special articles
in:

SMITH, W., WAYTE, WM., MARINDIN, G. E., *A Dictionary
of Greek and Roman Antiquities*[3]. 2 vols. London,
1914,

but to such reference books as:

JONES, H. STUART, *Companion to Roman History.* Oxford, 1912.

SANDYS, J. E., *A Companion to Latin Studies*[3]. Cam-
bridge, England, 1921.

The translation of L. A. Magnus, J. H. Freese and A.
B. Gough makes available the highly important work of
L. Friedländer, *Darstellungen aus der Sittengeschichte
Roms in der Zeit von August bis zum Ausgang der An-
tonine*[7], Leipzig, 1901, under the title *Roman Life and
Manners under the Early Empire.* 4 vols. London and
New York, 1908–1913.

Other comprehensive accounts are found in:

BECKER, W. A., *Gallus*[3], translated by F. Metcalfe. London, 1866. (New edition of the German, by H. Göll,
2 vols. Berlin, 1880–1882.)

DILL, S., *Roman Society from Nero to Marcus Aurelius*[2].
London, 1919.

BIBLIOGRAPHY

FOWLER, W. W., *Social Life at Rome in the Age of Cicero*. New York, 1909.

GUHL, E., and KONER, W., *Das Leben der Griechen und Römer*[6], herausgegeben von R. Engelmann, Berlin, 1893; translated from German 3d. Ed., by F. Hueffer. London, 1875.

JOHNSTON, H. W., *The Private Life of the Romans*. Chicago, 1903.

PRESTON, H. W., and DODGE, L., *The Private Life of the Romans*. Chicago, 1919. (Notable especially is the chapter on agriculture.)

THOMAS, É., *Roman Life under the Caesars*. (English Translation) New York, 1899.

TUCKER, T. G., *Life in the Roman World of Nero and St. Paul*. London, 1910.

Nor should one overlook certain essays in:

ABBOTT, F. F., *The Common People of Ancient Rome*. New York, 1911. *Society and Politics in Ancient Rome*. New York, 1909.

BAILEY, C., (Editor) *The Legacy of Rome*. Oxford, 1923.

Much interesting matter is scattered through the work of:

FRANK, T., *An Economic History of Rome*. Baltimore, 1920.

For Pompeii, the reader may be referred to:

GUSMAN, P., *Pompeii, the city, its life and art*, translated by F. Simmonds and M. Jourdain. London, 1900.

MAU, A., *Pompeii: Its Life and Art*[2], translated by F. W. Kelsey. New York and London, 1904. (Professor Kelsey has in preparation a new edition of this indispensable work for English readers.)

Easily accessible for pictures of many objects mentioned in this book are:

SCHREIBER, T., *Atlas of Classical Antiquities*. London, 1895.

and the

British Museum Guide to the Exhibition illustrating Greek and Roman Life. London, 1920.

[203]

Our Debt to Greece and Rome

AUTHORS AND TITLES

AUTHORS AND TITLES

AESCHYLUS AND SOPHOCLES. *J. T. Sheppard.*

GREEK RELIGION. *Walter Woodburn Hyde.*

SURVIVALS OF ROMAN RELIGION. *Gordon J. Laing.*

MYTHOLOGY. *Jane Ellen Harrison.*

ANCIENT BELIEFS IN THE IMMORTALITY OF THE SOUL. *Clifford H. Moore.*

STAGE ANTIQUITIES. *James Turney Allen.*

PLAUTUS AND TERENCE. *Gilbert Norwood.*

ROMAN POLITICS. *Frank Frost Abbott.*

PSYCHOLOGY, ANCIENT AND MODERN. *G. S. Brett.*

ANCIENT AND MODERN ROME. *Rodolfo Lanciani.*

WARFARE BY LAND AND SEA. *Eugene S. McCartney.*

THE GREEK FATHERS. *James Marshall Campbell.*

GREEK BIOLOGY AND MEDICINE. *Henry Osborn Taylor.*

MATHEMATICS. *David Eugene Smith.*

LOVE OF NATURE AMONG THE GREEKS AND ROMANS. *H. R. Fairclough.*

ANCIENT WRITING AND ITS INFLUENCE. *B. L. Ullman.*

GREEK ART. *Arthur Fairbanks.*

ARCHITECTURE. *Alfred M. Brooks.*

ENGINEERING. *Alexander P. Gest.*

MODERN TRAITS IN OLD GREEK LIFE. *Charles Burton Gulick.*

ROMAN PRIVATE LIFE. *Walton Brooks McDaniel.*

GREEK AND ROMAN FOLKLORE. *William Reginald Halliday.*

ANCIENT EDUCATION. *J. F. Dobson.*